JUST TO

Behold

Becoming Beautiful From the Inside Out

ANDREA T. ARNOLD

MYND
MATTERS

Just To Behold: Becoming Beautiful From the Inside Out
Copyright © 2022 by Andrea T. Arnold.

For permission requests and bulk orders, contact the author at www.justbeyoutifulproject.com.

Scripture taken from the New King James Version® of The Holy Bible. Copyright © 1982 by Thomas Nelson, Inc. Used by permission.

Mynd Matters Publishing
715 Peachtree Street NE
Suites 100 & 200
Atlanta, GA 30308

ISBN: 978-1-957092-05-8

To beautiful and special YOU,
Because you deserve to be acknowledged.

TO

_____

FROM

_____

DATE

_____

I don't profess to know everything, heck, I don't even profe..
know much of anything. I do, however, know how to enjoy
how to accept who I am and how to live my life unapologeti...
Why live on this earth and be miserable, unhappy, unloved, nu...
It's time to look in the mirror pick yourself up by your boot s...
and enjoy who you are. Life is meant to be lived, and life sh...
be full of love, happiness, and hopefulness. That way, we ca...
an inspiration to others and encourage them. Don't let anothe...
pass you by that isn't peaceful. Now this sounds too good ...
true, but the truth is, while we will have off-days, more importa...
we can all have more on-days than off. I detail how in my jour...

Just to Behold is not about my life; it's about what I have experie...
and how I coped. I want to encourage you to be you and enjoy
life to the fullest. Smile every chance you get, whether you
like it or not. Smile at the good and the bad, smile at the ups...
the downs, smile at the ins and the outs. Most of all, smile a...
successes and the failures. Look at everything as a lesson a...
stepping stone to get you to where you need to be. Don't let any...

Just to Behold

a daily confession

I am a beautiful woman, that accomplishes beautiful things.

I do not look like what I have been through.

I stand everyday with a bold beautiful confidence.

My beauty is woven into every fiber of my being.

I am a unique beauty.

I have a beautiful purpose.

I have a beautiful peace.

I have a beautiful smile.

I have a beautiful joy.

I exude beauty through and through that overflows daily.

No one can speak my beauty away.

No one can look my beauty away.

I am a beautiful woman from my hair follicles to my toenails and

their is no situation and no one that can change my beauty.

My beauty is so deeply rooted within me
I shall not be moved.

I am beautiful because I CHOOSE ME!

Introduction

For all the promises of God in Him are Yes,
and in Him Amen, to the glory of God through us.
- 2 Corinthians 1:20

The journal you have in your hands is not one to be read in order from front to back. This journal is meant to be read whereever you are in your life. Our lives take on many stages and this journal is designed just for that. Don't take this journal as ordinary. If you truly read and write as I have over the years, your life will change and you will be encouraged. We all are at different places in our lives and there is something here for each and every stage of your life's journey. So now is the time to get that cup of tea, coffee or whatever you prefer. Get in a quiet place to be able to pray, listen and write what God is speaking to you. We all have to start somewhere, so why not start where these pages fall open? Enjoy your journey and be blessed through the tears and through the smiles. You deserve to live a life of freedom and encouragement.

As you go through the pages, remember, everything in this journal is between you and God. Write down every prayer, every thought, every high note, every disappointment, etc. and always date your writings. Putting a date to your writings and reflections will encourage you when it comes to pass. Do not put a due date on God because we are on God's timing and not our own. Allow patience, faith, trust and love to overflow and overtake you during these times. God is a sovereign God and His promises are always, "Yes," and "Amen." Remember that He will never let you down and He is right there beside you, listening and reading every word you write. Be encouraged and always smile through everything in your life.

Heart's Desire for My Life

Before you start to flip through the pages of this journal, it's time to pray, seek and write down your heart's desire for your life. During this time do not let fear keep you from what God promised you. Be truthful with yourself. This is between you and God.

_____

_____

_____

_____

_____

_____

_____

_____

_____

_____

_____

_____

_____

_____

_____

_____

_____

Date

It's Personal

Forgiveness is Necessary

It is time to do some house cleaning and uprooting in our lives. Don't wait 'til spring to start cleaning out those areas in your life. Start now! There is a spirit of unforgiveness that has been roaming this earth too long and now is the time to stop that spirit in its tracks and destroy it at the root. Don't go another day with unforgiveness in your heart. We all need to start by acknowledging the unforgiveness, then repenting for the spirit of unforgiveness, and then releasing whomever you are holding hostage by your attitude of unforgiveness. What is it profiting you to hold unforgiveness in your heart toward your fellow man? Unforgiveness is a silent killer: it will stunt your spiritual growth, it will block your peace, it will block your success, and it will cause blockages in every area of your life. I can't understand how we can hold unforgiveness toward each other on this earth when we mess up royally many times with our Lord and Savior Jesus Christ! And He still forgives us many times over. Come on and let it go!!! Unforgiveness is a heart issue because it gets rooted in the heart so deep for so long. When roots remain for a period of time it takes more strength to uproot them. Don't continue allowing the spirit of unforgiveness to grow deep roots in your heart. It's time to release and uproot whatever has you not wanting to let go of unforgiveness toward anyone. *And be ye kind one to another, tenderhearted, forgiving one another, even as God for Christ's sake hath forgiven you. Eph. 4:32.* One way to help with unforgiveness is communication. People don't want to communicate and if we look close enough, it's because of pride. You cannot live on this earth day in and day out and not communicate with one other. I'm not perfect, we are not perfect. One thing that's for sure — we can ask God to reveal to us areas in our lives that need to be perfected. Let's not go another day with a spirit of unforgiveness and holding others hostage because of how we feel. Get up out of yourself, let go of your pride, let go of how you thought a situation should have gone, let go of hurting yourself each and every day by harboring those feelings and FORGIVE!!! You want a life free in Christ, at peace in Christ and joyful in Christ? Then start to uproot that spirit of unforgiveness in your heart. You are a beautiful daughter of the Most High and now is the time to live like it. Start today making the first step toward your freedom and forgive. Make sure before you leave that house today, you look in that mirror and give yourself the biggest smile! Always remember, no matter what, to share that unique smile with yourself first and then others who cross your path today.

Journal Time

Now is the time to get quiet before God and pray. Write a confession for God to give you a heart of forgiveness towards yourself and others. Be truthful with yourself. This is between you and God.

_____

_____

_____

_____

_____

_____

_____

_____

_____

_____

_____

_____

_____
Date

Trust Yourself

Trusting yourself is one key to enjoying your life. You know we are our own worst enemy if we really look at it from an inner perspective. That is why we need to truly understand who and whose we are and to be honest with ourselves. We can do so much more in our lives than we even give ourselves credit for. Start today by changing how you see yourself and build up your confidence in Jesus Christ to trust who you are. Others opinions of you doesn't matter. What matters most is that you trust yourself enough to believe that you can have a wonderful life. I am not talking about money, success, work, etc. I am talking about life; the life you have been blessed to live. Most of all is to know that you can have the best life right now and go for it. Life is too short to miss the best opportunities because of negative vibes and distractions. The most important thing to remember is that your past does not define who you are. Your mistakes in life do not determine who you are. It's time to get healed of the guilt and the shame of your past and move forward in a solid confidence of who you are in Christ Jesus. You were created for a purpose for such a time as this and no one or nothing can take that from you. Guard your identity in Christ Jesus and do not let situations steal who you were purposed to be. Now is the time. Yes, right now, to get up, show up, dress up and get your life back on purpose and enjoy every breath you breathe. You have a right to be you because you were created in the image of God and your Heavenly Father hand-picked you for this season on this earth. Don't let another day pass you by that you doubt who you are. I warn you to not let pride overtake you as you walk confidently. Stay humble in Christ Jesus and walk with a quiet confidence of who you are. Trust me, that will speak loudly than anything else when you walk in a room. The enemy will know who and whose you are. Trust yourself daily and don't doubt who you were created to be. You are your own unique person with your own unique style. Don't try and mirror someone else because that is not you. We are all different. Just find your uniqueness and go with the flow in Christ Jesus. Always remember, no matter what, to share that unique smile with yourself first and then others who cross your path today.

Now is the time to get quiet before God and pray. Write a confession for God to give you a heart of forgiveness towards yourself and others. Be truthful with yourself. This is between you and God.

_____

_____

_____

_____

_____

_____

_____

_____

_____

_____

_____

_____

_____

_____

_____

_____

_____
Date

Watch What You Speak to Yourself

New week, new victories! Let's prepare today for an awesome week ahead. Just know that you are important in God's eyes. You are a woman who has authority to speak into your life and situations. Do not allow your situations to dictate your life. Do not allow words spoken over you (whether you heard them or not) to dictate who you are. Don't even allow yourself to speak negative words over who you are. You are more than enough, you are a conqueror, you are loved, you are the daughter of the Most High. Let no one tell you otherwise. Take a stand against the enemy and let him know that none of his weapons formed against you shall prosper because greater is in you than he that is in this world. Woman of God, you are somebody and now is the time to walk like it, talk like it, think like it and build up your most holy confidence daily, and be about your life and purpose. God handpicked you for such a time and season as this. Do not get distracted and influenced by anyone or any situation. Stay the course that God has strategically prepared and designed for your life. You see we are all different, with different purposes, but one thing for sure we have a common goal. Trust who you are because you are God's precious treasure and don't let the enemy steal your jewels. Make it a goal this week to walk daily with a spiritual confidence of who you are in Christ Jesus. Have a wonderful day headed for a wonderful week, to a wonderful month, to a wonderful year. Always remember, no matter what, share that unique smile with yourself first and then others that cross your path today.

Love Yourself, Be Kind to Yourself & Watch Your Words You Are Listening.

Now is the time to get quiet before God and pray. Write a prayer to ask God to allow you to see yourself through His eyes. Be truthful with yourself. This is between you and God.

_____

_____

_____

_____

_____

_____

_____

_____

_____

_____

_____

_____

_____

Date

Just a Cup

Just a cup will do. Some of us wake up every morning filling up our favorite cup with coffee or tea just to get our day started. Why not wake up every morning first filling up your spiritual cup with just what you need for the day? Your cup can only hold so much, but oh, what can overflow will bless your day and those around you. You can carry that spiritual cup with you all day long and it will stay the right temperature and never weaken in satisfaction. It will always be the right amount of whatever you need for the day. You may ask what could be in your cup? Well, we could sip a cup of joy that could carry you through the day or a gulp of love 'cause we all need just a little more love toward ourselves and others. Maybe, it's a sip of faith 'cause we need to believe for God's awesome power to shine down on a situation. Whatever is in your cup, just sip it slowly throughout the day and enjoy. Every day you awaken, fill your cup up with just what you need for the day to carry you through and watch how awesome your day is, even if it gets turned upside down. All we need is a cup; just a cup of what God ordered for us. You see, it doesn't take much to enjoy life when we spend that quality time with Jesus. If you haven't ordered yet, it's not too late 'cause just a spiritual cup will do. Have an awesome day in Christ Jesus. Always remember, no matter what, share that unique smile with yourself first and then others that cross your path today.

*All you need is a drop of what
God has ordered for your day.
So fill your spiritual cup daily.*

Now is the time to get quiet before God and pray. Write a prayer for God to fill your cup to overflowing with just the right amount of what you need in your life. Be truthful with yourself. This is between you and God.

_____

_____

_____

_____

_____

_____

_____

_____

_____

_____

_____

_____

_____

_____

Date

Just Be

Don't doubt where you are in life at this moment. We must remember that our Heavenly Father has a specific plan for each and every one of us and sometimes, He has to get our attention. Don't be discouraged because of where your life is at this moment. As you read this, just know that where you are right now is necessary for your life and your destiny. When a train goes off track it has no other option but to stop because there is no way for it to keep going until it is put back on track. Same way in our lives. We will go off track just so God can get our attention.

Often we feel like our life is on a merry-go-round, stuck going round and round. Just know it is necessary to be where you are. Don't move prematurely before you work out anything that will hinder your future. We can't take bad worn out baggage to the next level. Allow yourself to be right where you are and most importantly, learn from every experience. Life is a lesson, so learn it well and don't ever forget no matter how hard it is, ENJOY where you are on the way to where you are headed. Better days are in front of you. Don't forget to smile at yourself first and let that smile overflow onto someone else that crosses your path today. Always remember, no matter what, share that unique smile with yourself first and then others that cross your path today.

Allow yourself to be right where you are.

Make a list of what helps you to be content. Be truthful with yourself. This is between you and God.

_____

_____

_____

_____

_____

_____

_____

_____

_____

_____

_____

_____

_____

_____

_____

_____
Date

Your Attitude Matters

It's time to adjust our attitude in every part of our lives. Don't pick and choose your attitude toward yourself, others, situations, etc. We must have the same attitude for everything in life. Your attitude determines how you will react to situations, experiences and people. It's time to make a true attitude adjustment and stay consistent and positive in your mindset. One bad attitude can throw off your whole day, hour, minute, second or life. Don't let a bad attitude distance you from the people that God has placed in your life for such a time as this. You see, God may place others on your path not for themselves, but for you. The question is, how will your attitude be? Don't fake a false attitude. Eventually the true attitude you hold inside will come to light. We have no excuses now to make that attitude right. One way to start to change that attitude is to spend quality time in prayer, examine yourself, repent, and think differently. Get up every morning and throughout the day and confess over yourself: "I have a new mindset that will lead to a right attitude." We are in this together for the long haul, so let's strap ourselves in and reach higher heights because we got this. God is on our side and we have each other. Have a wonderful day. Go out and share your positive attitude with the world and share a smile because we all need one. Always remember, no matter what, share that unique smile with yourself first and then others that cross your path today.

If you want to soar to new heights then adjust your attitude and rise.

Make a list of where your attitude needs to be adjusted. Be truthful with yourself. This is between you and God.

_____

_____

_____

_____

_____

_____

_____

_____

_____

_____

_____

_____

_____

_____

_____

_____

_____

_____
Date

I Choose to Be Happy

Everyday we wake up with choices and one thing for sure is that one of our choices needs to be choosing to BE HAPPY! Choosing to be happy in your life will take you further than you can even imagine. When you create a life that overflows with happiness and a positive mindset, then all the negative distractions coming your way will only be a blur and insignificant. We must live a life with a smile on our face, a skip in our step and share the love of Jesus Christ. I have realized that no matter what I am facing, as long as I am happy and looking for the best of every situation and sharing love with others, I can look forward to tomorrow. Stop focusing on the situations that aren't benefiting you or your future and focus on what gets results. We need to reprogram our mindset so that we can live a happy life in Christ Jesus. Don't forget: people, money, success, and things don't make us truly happy. These are only temporary happiness-makers. What makes us truly happy daily is knowing the love of God and who we are and our purpose. Set goals in your life to confess over yourself daily to remind yourself where your true happiness comes from. Make it a goal and choice today to BE HAPPY and watch how your day goes. Always remember, no matter what, share that unique smile with yourself first and then others that cross your path today.

Today I choose happiness.

Make a list of areas in your life to de clutter to make your days more at peace and joyful. Be truthful with yourself. This is between you and God.

_____

_____

_____

_____

_____

_____

_____

_____

_____

_____

_____

_____

_____

_____

_____

_____

_____

Date

Be the Light

We must live our lives every day making sure we are the light shining through the darkness. We need to constantly be the light on the hill. When ships are lost at sea, they usually have a lighthouse that guides them to safety. Work on being that lighthouse in people's lives that can guide the way to safety in Christ Jesus. Some people are so lost and so far in their mess that they only see darkness. This is why we need to be that shimmer of light that can give them the hope they need to come back to life. Stop being so caught up in your own life and shine brighter than ever before. When we all shine our lights at a high voltage, what a peaceful, blessed world we can live in. The light will outshine the darkness every time. People cross our paths every day that need a light to shine in their life. When we allow our light to shine brightly it not only gives us a hope and a confidence that we can make it, but also it will give others a glimpse of hope that nothing is impossible. Don't allow yourself, situations or others to dim your light. It's time to start today shining bright because you are the light of the world. Get up, start your day in prayer and shine as bright as you can because you deserve to shine! I challenge you today to share your light! Always remember, no matter what, share that unique smile with yourself first and then others that cross your path today.

Let your light shine daily for all to see and experience.

Now is the time to get quiet before God and pray. Write a prayer to ask God to allow your light to shine daily. Be truthful with yourself. This is between you and God.

_____

_____

_____

_____

_____

_____

_____

_____

_____

_____

_____

_____

_____

_____

_____

_____
Date

Adjust Your Mindset

Our mindset determines how we live. When our mindset is toxic, our lives are toxic. We must make an effort daily to have a mindset that we find in Philippians 4:8, "whatever things are true, whatever things are noble, whatever things are just, whatever things are pure, whatever things are lovely, whatever things are of good report, if there is any virtue and if there is anything praiseworthy—meditate on these things." When we think on these things, then we don't have time to think on anything opposite of what we've just confessed. Now, this is not easy when we live in a world of chaos, confusion & hate, but it's not impossible. Just like we have to discipline our lives to be healthy by exercising, we must discipline our minds to be positive by "exercising" positive thoughts & confessions on a daily basis. Don't get discouraged. This will take time. If we start by ignoring the negative thoughts, we will start to change our mindset one positive thought at a time. Let's start today making a strong effort to think differently and change our mindset for the better so that we live a life fulfilled. Focus on what's positive and peaceful. Enjoy your life and spread the joy to someone else. Love yourself first today so that you may share love with others. Always remember, no matter what, share that unique smile with yourself first and then others that cross your path today.

Mindset is Everything.
You have the option to choose
how you live your life daily.

28

Make a list of what to meditate on daily. Be truthful with yourself. This is between you and God.

_____

_____

_____

_____

_____

_____

_____

_____

_____

_____

_____

_____

_____

_____

_____

_____
Date

Disconnect

This one word spoke volumes to me and I just want to share what I heard. Sometimes we have to disconnect from what is not benefitting our well-being. We need to disconnect from social media; disconnect from friends and associates who are bringing us grief; disconnect from conversations that have no substance; disconnect from that man we think is "the one;" disconnect from fear of what's holding us back; disconnect from lack; disconnect from business; and disconnect from exhaustion. I could go on and on, but look at it this way, disconnect from that bad power source and get connected to the Power that can change your life around for the best. It's never too late to make a move in the right direction. Do something today that can get you plugged into the right source (Jesus) so that you can glow on. Always remember, no matter what, share that unique smile with yourself first and then others that cross your path today.

Disconnect in order to connect to God.

Make a list — no matter how hard or impossible it seems — of who and what you need to disconnect from. Be truthful with yourself. This is between you and God.

_____

_____

_____

_____

_____

_____

_____

_____

_____

_____

_____

_____

_____

_____

_____

_____

_____

Date

Today's Mood

Let's not forget to start our day off with a double dose of spending time with Jesus and then, perhaps, a sip of coffee. You know sometimes we spend our lives getting so busy and caught up in mundane routines that we stop doing first things first. It's time to push pause and push restart in our lives. One important part of our life is prayer and some of us (including me) need to recharge and get back to the basics. You don't have to spend hours in prayer, but make sure that the time you spend is quality prayer time. Start your day off when you open your eyes in prayer and watch how your day goes. Now don't get me wrong, you will still have challenges during the day, but think how much stronger you will be to face them. It's better to be ready than to get ready. Make today a good one and enjoy your life to the fullest. Always remember, no matter what, share that unique smile with yourself first and then others that cross your path today.

Today's good mood is sponsored by:
Jesus & coffee or tea.

Start your day off by writing down a simple prayer that can carry you through the rest of the day no matter what comes your way.

_____

_____

_____

_____

_____

_____

_____

_____

_____

_____

_____

_____

_____

_____

_____

_____

_____
Date

Hold On: God is Not Done

I am here to tell you God is not done with you yet. There is so much more that He needs you to do. All He is asking is for you to get in place, prepare yourself in prayer and to spend quality time with Him and listen. We must learn to ignore the noise and listen to that still small voice. There is such a greater work to be done and He is preparing you for that work as you read this encouragement. Do not continue to ignore what you know God has told you and showed you. Running only causes a life out of control. Get control and take back who and whose you are. Don't be afraid to leap into God's plan for your life and your destiny. So much greater God has placed inside of you. Now is the time to exercise your gifts. God has given you just what He knew you could handle. If God trusted you with your gift then you need to trust God with your life. Stop fearing and exercise what we all have: faith. He has given each one of us a measure of faith to walk life's journey. Get up off that seat and go!

Situations that aren't benefitting your life are just noise. What is noise? Noise is anything other than what is of God and His purpose and plan in your life. Noise keeps you from hearing clearly. Noise keeps you distracted and unfocused. Noise stunts your spiritual growth. Get past the noise and get to the peace in your life. Stop letting your mind and what you see in the natural dictate your life. It's time to not only get rid of the noise, but to acquire 20/20 vision. We are coming into a year of 20/20 and God is saying it's time to see clearly now. The rain is gone. Stop trying to focus a blurred mindset because of what you may think it is. It's time to go to the Great Physician and say, "Lord, I need my 20/20 vision back because I need to be able to spiritually see everything You need me to see to carry out the purpose and plan that you have for me. Repent of your blurred outlook on life and let God give you a new vision with no glasses needed or surgery to correct it. All you need is a touch and your sight will be restored.

Stop holding yourself and others hostage because of how you thought a situation turned out. You see, we have people in our lives for a season and a reason. Maybe that season was for one hour, one day or it could be that those people are in your life for a lifetime. Whatever the situation, stop looking at others with your fleshly eyes and distorted mindset. You are only hurting yourself because they have moved on and you are sitting there looking like the world has done you wrong. People are there for tests and lessons. Iron sharpens iron. Do not let a situation where you are supposed to be sharpening iron together and one little situation happens and their sharp iron has dulled a side of yours. That is unforgiveness. There's no such thing as I-will-forgive-you-but-I-won't-forget. If you keep going through life with that same mentality every time a person walks out of your life, you'll only add another bag of unforgiveness onto your back. Forgive and forget is the only way. When we think about everything we have done to our Heavenly Father, He forgave us and threw it into the sea of forgetfulness. Then who are we that we are so much more mighty to hold onto every grudge and wrong that has ever been done to us?

Come on, it's time to rise up spiritually and be the woman of God He has created you to be. God may even put someone in your life that acts just like you to show you, you, since you wouldn't take the time to get in that mirror one-on-one with yourself and spend time with God to find out what He really needed to tell you. So slow down before you get in the dangerous place of judging someone else because it very well could be you one-on-one without the mirror. Time is moving quickly and we don't have much longer on this earth. The question is, "What will you do from this day forward to share what God has called you to do?" Stop hesitating because you're looking at that bank account. As long as the enemy can keep you looking at "noise" in your bank account when in actuality you have everything you already need, then you will stay right where you are and not move forward. Stop looking at your life as what you think it is and look beyond at what it is. Always remember, no matter what, share that unique smile with yourself first and then others that cross your path today.

The past is your lesson. The present is your gift. The future is your motivation.

Choices: Choose Wisely

Life is full of choices every second, every minute, every hour. That is why it is so crucial to wake up early and get before God so that you can make right and sound choices. In life we won't always make every right choice, but I thank my God that He gives us a portion of grace and mercy to carry us through whatever choice we make. Don't beat yourself up over a not so quite right choice you made. Just make sure that if you make the wrong choice, run quickly to your Heavenly Father, repent, and get the choice right. Embrace your choices in life because they are there to grow and mature you on this journey of life. We are not perfect and we won't always get it right, but the key is to know when you haven't gotten it right. Quickly fall to your knees and ask God for guidance. Step out today with a confidence that whatever choices come your way, you will decide wisely. Always remember, no matter what, share that unique smile with yourself first and then others that cross your path today.

Every day you have the power to choose,
so choose wisely and stand firm in your choice.

Make a list of choices that you need to correct, repent and pray that God gives you an opportunity to get it right. Be truthful with yourself. This is between you and God.

_____

_____

_____

_____

_____

_____

_____

_____

_____

_____

_____

_____

_____

_____

_____

_____

_____
Date

Hold Tight

An unchanging God with an unchanging purpose. God does not change and His purpose does not change, but we are so busy in our mindset trying to understand what happened. What changed? The clear answer is we changed. We got influenced along the way; we just got completely off track. Now, God is trying to nudge us back on that track of purpose in our lives. One thing's for sure, while He is nudging you, do not go against Him. God is trying to get your attention and save your life. Just get up, dust yourself off and rid of the guilt and shame. Get yourself back on that track destined for purpose and roll on toward your destiny. God is calling each and every one of us back into His unchanging purpose and plan. It's time to wake up because the spiritual alarm clock is ringing and only those with open minds and hearts will hear. If you stay ready, you don't have to get ready. Don't stay asleep, but awaken and rise to the sound of God's Holy calling in your life. Trust who you are because you are God's precious treasure. Don't let the enemy steal your jewels. Have a wonderful day headed for a wonderful week. Always remember, no matter what, share that unique smile with yourself first and then others that cross your path today.

Hold on to God's unchanging hand.

Now is the time to get quiet before God and pray. Write a prayer for God to give you the strength to hold tight to His hand. Be truthful with yourself. This is between you and God.

_____

_____

_____

_____

_____

_____

_____

_____

_____

_____

_____

_____

_____

_____

_____

_____

Date

Refocus and Make a Difference

We need to refocus our why, what and how in life. Success and money is good, but some questions to ask yourself:

- **Why am I on this earth?**
- **What is my reason for waking up every day?**
- **How am I making a difference daily?**

I believe that life's fulfillment is helping others even if it's a simple smile or hello. We have lost our why, what and how by being focused on the things that can be lost in a second. Don't get so caught up in your daily routine that you forget to spread a little ray of sunlight to someone else. We never know what that person beside us is going through or what they are on the brink of (and you don't need to know!) All you need to do is smile and say, "Hello!" Which will go a long way and last more than success or wealth. Always remember, no matter what, share that unique smile with yourself first and then others that cross your path today.

Make it a goal today:
To spread a little love in someone's
direction and give people hope
that there are others in this
world today that still care.

Now is the time to get quiet before God and pray. Write a list of how you can make a daily difference in the world.

_____

_____

_____

_____

_____

_____

_____

_____

_____

_____

_____

_____

_____

_____

_____

_____
Date

Hold Tight to Who You Are

Today is a day to walk out that door into the world ready and confident for whatever is coming your way. You are a daughter of the Most High God and nothing is impossible. Everything is possible! You woke up with a gift this morning and that is the breath of life. God saw fit today to wake you up this morning 'cause there is still a greater work to be done here on this earth. Keep your spiritual eyes open and spiritual ears listening to see what your mission is for today. Every day we wake up we need to ask God, "what will you have me do today to share Your love and encouragement with someone else?" As you walk out that door you walk in confidence today, you walk in peace today, you walk in love today, you walk in joy today, you walk in favor today and speak life all day long. No matter what comes your way you flash that smile and say to yourself, "I got this," because there is a greater One on the inside of me and I shall not be moved. Walk on to greatness! My sister, you are special, you are loved, you are healed, you are free and there is nothing and no one that can take that from you unless you allow it. So hold tight to who and whose you are and don't let go because your life depends on it. Always remember, no matter what, share that unique smile with yourself first and then others that cross your path today. Be blessed and carry on!!!

The best project you will ever work on is your self.

Make a list of encouragements to speak over yourself. Be truthful with yourself. This is between you and God.

_____

_____

_____

_____

_____

_____

_____

_____

_____

_____

_____

_____

_____

_____

Date

Get Disciplined in Your Life

How do you start your day? Do you realize the same way you start your day is the same way you should end your day and all the time in between? It is a gift from God every morning that He allows you to open your eyes; so don't take it for granted. God should be first on your mind in the morning. Not reaching over for that cell phone to see who liked an Instagram post you posted yesterday; not checking Facebook to see who posted what they did the night before; not the remote control to see the latest weather or best route to get to work. No, you should be talking with God and letting Him talk to you. You may need a good strategy for the day because God knows what you are about to face before your feet even hit the floor. Stop sleeping your time away from God. Get disciplined in your life to commune with God daily. He misses some of us dearly and longs for those prayers from our heart. If we start our day off with God, then He walks and talks with us all day long. Don't miss another opportunity to be pleasing to your Heavenly Father. He is sitting right there waiting for you to open your heart and mouth and talk to Him. Other times He is just waiting for us to sit at His feet while He talks to us. We don't always have to be the one talking — sometimes we talk too much — we need to hush and listen to God. Always remember, no matter what, share that unique smile with yourself first and then others that cross your path today.

Rise up and pray daily for direction, encouragement and confirmation.

Now is the time to get quiet before God and pray. Start today by praying for daily discipline in your life. Be truthful with yourself. This is between you and God.

_____

_____

_____

_____

_____

_____

_____

_____

_____

_____

_____

_____

_____

_____

_____

Date

I Shall Not be Moved Today

Make every day you wake up worth it to be alive. We need to stop letting people move us and get us out of character. People will always be around to try us and bump our focus off of our purpose. I have learned in my life that I have enough confidence to know who I am and that I don't have to respond to the negative actions of others or to negative situations. Don't entertain negative actions because it profits you nothing. If I stay focused on why I am here on this earth then everything else is just a distraction. Make your life count and encourage someone else to enjoy the life they were blessed with. We have got to show love and compassion toward ourselves and toward others if we want to live a life in full bloom. Start today by making it a goal to not be moved by others or situations and to enjoy your life to the fullest. Today, let's take the focus off of us and do something for someone else even if it's a smile in passing. Always remember, no matter what, share that unique smile with yourself first and then others that cross your path today.

As long as you stay firmly planted in who and whose you are; you shall not be moved by what comes your way.

Start today by praying a simple prayer and asking God to make you steadfast in your reaction to others and situations. Be truthful with yourself. This is between you and God.

_____

_____

_____

_____

_____

_____

_____

_____

_____

_____

_____

_____

_____

Date

You are Called by Name

This is a time to humble your spirit, mind and heart. This is a time to get before God and cry out to Him in prayer. This is a time to open that dusty Bible and seek His face. This is a time to repent and tell the Lord you are ready to turn from what is not of Him. When we decide to truly do the Word of God in the order He says in 2 Chronicles 7:14, then God will hear our sincere cry and forgive us of all our sins. And today most importantly, heal our land. Oh, how our land needs to be healed. Right now, today, God is getting our attention. This is nothing new. God did it way back thousands of years ago when the earth was full of sin and disobedience. He created disasters to get people's attention. It's time to wake up and get your life back on track. The family needs to be restored. Our hearts need to be softened to one another as neighbors. We need to put our trust back into the one true God who sustains life. Don't take this time for granted, but take this time to return to your one true love, Jesus Christ. Just know, man and money cannot fix the broken land. Only God can heal and put together to make the land whole and complete. Get your life together, do the Word and most of all pray. I know they talk about social distancing, but never forget no matter how far apart we have to get, a smile can go a long way. Always remember, no matter what, share that unique smile with yourself first and then others that cross your path today.

If My people who are called by My name will humble themselves, and pray and seek My face, and turn from their wicked ways, then I will hear from heaven, and will forgive their sin and heal their land.
2 Chronicles 7:14

Now is the time to get quiet before God and pray. Write a prayer today by asking God to humble your spirit, mind and heart. Be truthful with yourself. This is between you and God.

_____

_____

_____

_____

_____

_____

_____

_____

_____

_____

_____

_____

_____

_____

_____

_____

_____
Date

Be Pleasing Where It Counts

It is time for us to get real and honest with ourselves. Too many days have gone by that we are pleasing to the wrong one. We need to take a pleasing inventory and see if we are pleasing those around us or if we are pleasing God. Pleasing people will cause us many heartaches both physically and mentally. Stop trying to get the approval of people and get the approval of God. Live your life every day pleasing God and being the apple of His eye. We need to stop depending so much on man to make situations happen in our lives, because 9 times out of 10, they will let us down. Every time. If you know who you truly are in God's eyes then nothing else or no one can influence you otherwise. God warns us in His Word that He will have no other gods before Him (Exodus 20:3). So, take heed and stop trying to get the approval of this world. What benefits can you receive from getting the approval of this world? None. Always remember, no matter what, share that unique smile with yourself first and then others that cross your path today.

That you may walk worthy of the Lord,
fully pleasing Him, being fruitful in
every good work and increasing
in the knowledge of God;
Colossians 1:10

50

Now is the time to get quiet before God and pray. Write a pleasing prayer to God and allow Him to commune with you.

_____

_____

_____

_____

_____

_____

_____

_____

_____

_____

_____

_____

_____

_____

_____

_____

_____
Date

You Have Everything You Need

Do you really know and understand how blessed you are? You are blessed more than you even know. You are important; you have a purpose and a place on this earth. It's time to speak to yourself and let yourself know that you are precious in God's eyes. You don't need approval from man or for man to tell you how precious you are. You were created in the image of God and He thought of you for such a time as this... right here in this moment He is thinking of you. You are not alone, you are not less than and you are not beneath anyone else. You are special, you are unique and you are you. Don't let anyone tell you differently.

Everything you need God has placed on the inside of you to live the best most enjoyable life you were gifted to live. Life is a gift and we need to treat it as the best gift we have ever received. You get up each and every day with a purpose to live, with a purpose to praise, with a purpose to pray, and watch what happens in your life. Learn to forgive yourself when you need to. Condition your mindset to think more encouraging thoughts toward yourself. Once you can appreciate who you are in Christ Jesus, then, and only then, can you learn and practice every day to treat others right. Love is the most precious and powerful action you could ever share with someone else. "For this is the message that you heard from the beginning, that we should love one another," 1 John 3:11.

Let's start right now by encouraging ourselves with love and sharing a smile every time we pass by that mirror because you look so much better when you smile. Once you've got it, then share that smile and love with someone else. Take the time today to call someone and encourage them because we all can use a little bit of encouragement. I am sharing a smile with you right now as you have read my heart. Have a peaceful, joyful and living day in Christ Jesus. May you and your families be blessed and safe. Always remember, no matter what, share that unique smile with yourself first and then others that cross your path today.

Now is the time to get quiet before God and pray. Write a thankful prayer for how God has kept you daily. Be truthful with yourself. This is between you and God.

_____

_____

_____

_____

_____

_____

_____

_____

_____

_____

_____

_____

_____

_____

_____
Date

Know Who You are with Confidence

Keep this as your peace of mind everyday:

You matter.
You're important.
You're loved.

And your presence on this earth makes a difference whether you see it or not. Live your life to the fullest because you are unique in every way. Don't let others discourage your uniqueness. There is no duplicate of you. You are one of a kind. Live your life unapologetically because you have a confidence knowing who you are. You are beautiful and don't let anyone take that from you. Be confident in knowing you are unique from the inside out. Get in a quiet space and let God minister to you who you are, how special you are and how much you are loved. Search the scriptures and start confessing over yourself who you were created to be. Don't sit during this time feeling alone, defeated, discouraged, fearful, and don't speak doubt over yourself. Lift yourself up with the Word of God and walk every day with confidence in knowing that you are a Child of God. Once you get this in your mindset, you can share it with someone else that needs to hear who they are in Christ Jesus. Smile at yourself and then share that smile with others. Always remember, no matter what, share that unique smile with yourself first and then others that cross your path today.

Now is the time to get quiet before God and pray. Write a prayer that God will reveal who He truly created you to be. Be truthful with yourself. This is between you and God.

_____

_____

_____

_____

_____

_____

_____

_____

_____

_____

_____

_____

_____

_____

_____

_____

_____
Date

Just Be Open

God puts people in our lives for a purpose and a season and we need to stay open to hear. When the time is right He will speak through them to us and He will not allow any interruptions to come when it is time. We may not understand why the times come as they do, but it is not for us to try and figure out, but to take in what the Lord is saying. It's a good thing to be able to sit and listen and take in that nugget. When He speaks it is not only encouraging, but the Lord is teaching us what He desires us to do right where we are. He knows one day we will be trading places with the person speaking to us and we will be His vessel encouraging someone else right where God has them. God is about timing and He has strategically timed everything to fall right into place when the time is right. When we are open to receive and begin to be obedient to what thus says the Lord. Don't operate in a hesitant spirit, but also don't do things 'cause you think that is what you ought to be doing. With God, just walk the best way you know how at the time no matter what is going on in or around you. Hear what the Lord is speaking and obey, start walking diligently in what He gives you for such a time as this. Always remember, no matter what, share that unique smile with yourself first and then others that cross your path today.

Be not forgetful to entertain strangers: for thereby some have entertained angels unawares.
Hebrews 13:2

Now is the time to get quiet before God and pray. Write a confession for God to help you be open towards yourself and others. Be truthful with yourself. This is between you and God.

_____

_____

_____

_____

_____

_____

_____

_____

_____

_____

_____

_____

_____

_____

_____

_____

_____

Date

Draw Close to God

Now is not the time to keep God at 6-ft. in our lives. We are hearing over and over and over again to social distance, keep at least 6-ft. between you and others. That is fine for our health and safety, but this does not pertain to God. We need to make sure daily we are not social distancing from God. It is easy to keep God at 6-ft. in our lives these days with all the headlines, the lies, the confusion, the sickness, the deaths, or the hard decisions we are having to make day in and day out. God is saying, "if you keep me at 6-ft. then I can't do what I need to do on your behalf. I need to be so close to you in a time like this that nothing can separate us. My Word says let nothing separate you from the love of God. I need you right now today to hold to My unchanging hand so tight that no hurt, harm or danger can come nigh your dwelling. Don't get so down and discouraged that you distance yourself from Me because you think I have forgotten about you or I am not working on your behalf. I will always be a way maker, promise keeper, light in the darkness, ... because that is who I AM."

Let today be the day that if you have social distanced from God that you will draw near to God like never before. It is getting ready to get worse before it gets better. But the good news is we can live our lives in the better right now because God our Father is holding us in the palm of His hand. He is telling us as you read this that, "I am with you like I have always been; don't look for Me at a distance. Look at Me as being right beside you like footprints in the sand which only has one set because I am carrying you through every circumstance in your life. Always, remember even though you may not see me, I am with you in the trees that reach toward the heavens, in the birds that sing My praises in the morning, in the flowers that bloom to show My beauty, in the wind that blows with My still small voice through the earth. If you listen close enough you can hear My instructions for your life to carry you through for what is ahead. Be encouraged and don't let go of My unchanging hand for I am with you always if you look for Me."

Be encouraged today like never before and let us draw closer to our Heavenly Father together. Pick yourself up and remain up because greater is He that is in you than he that is in the world and we have nothing and no one to fear. Carry on in a peaceful, blessed and worshipful day today. Always remember, no matter what, to share that unique smile with yourself first and then others that cross your path today.

Journal Time

Now is the time to get quiet before God and pray. Write a prayer to remain close to God daily. Be truthful with yourself. This is between you and God.

_____

_____

_____

_____

_____

_____

_____

_____

_____

_____

_____

_____

Date

Be Consistent

The word for today is consistency. Ladies, it is time to be consistent in our lives. If we want to be changed from the inside out we must be consistent to follow through no matter how difficult and real it can get. Change is not something you say and "poof" it happens. It is an action that takes consistency daily. It's time to get up every morning and speak over yourself who you are and what you can accomplish. If you truly desire something you put your all into it to make it happen. Let wanting to be changed from the inside out be something you can't live without and go for it. You have so much potential on the inside of you that needs to be brought to the surface. Don't waste another day wishing and wanting. Take time today to write down your heart's desire for yourself. Then spend time every day being consistent to make a change in your life. I just thought I would take the time to encourage you today and share where I am in being consistent with my purpose. I also wanted to share a personal smile with you today. Always, remember, no matter what, to share that unique smile with yourself first and then others that cross your path today.

Consistency and Discipline is more important than Perfection.

Make a list of things that will help you be and remain consistent in your life daily. Be truthful with yourself. This is between you and God.

_____

_____

_____

_____

_____

_____

_____

_____

_____

_____

_____

_____

_____

_____

_____

_____
Date

Beautiful in His Time

God has truly made all things beautiful in His time and the exciting part to that is it includes you. Just as the butterfly has to go through a transformation process to come into its true beauty, so do you. Stay in that cocoon as long as needed, but not past your time to come out as the beautiful person God created you to be. Don't fear your beauty, embrace who you are from the inside out. You are not alone. We are in this journey of life together. Let's start today and support, encourage and inspire each other to be beautiful from the inside out. Always remember, no matter what, to share that unique smile with yourself first and then others that cross your path today.

He has made everything beautiful in its time.
Also He has put eternity in their hearts,
except that no one can find out the work that
God does from beginning to end.
Ecclesiastes 3:11

Now is the time to get quiet before God and pray. Write a prayer asking God to keep you patient until He sees fit. Be truthful with yourself. This is between you and God.

_____

_____

_____

_____

_____

_____

_____

_____

_____

_____

_____

_____

_____

_____

_____

Date

Aspire to Inspire

Turn Off the Noise

We have too much noise in our lives and it is time to turn off the noise and hear clearly. It's time to change your mindset and get a renewed mind in Christ Jesus so that your spiritual hearing is clear. We must come to understand that the situations that aren't benefitting our lives is just noise. What is noise you may ask? Noise is anything other than what is of God and His purpose and plan for your life. Noise keeps you from hearing clearly. Noise keeps you distracted and unfocused. Noise can stunt your spiritual growth. It is time to get past the noise and get to the peace in your life. Stop letting your mindset and what you see in the natural dictate your life. It's time to not only get rid of the noise, but to acquire clear hearing. God is saying it's time to hear clearly now that the noise is gone. Stop trying to focus on a blurred mindset because of what you may think it is. It's time to go to the Great Physician and say, "Lord, I need my clear, noise-free hearing back cause I need to be able to hear spiritually everything You need me to hear to carry out the purpose and plan that you have for my life. Repent of your noisy outlook on life and let God give you new hearing with no hearing aid or surgery needed to correct it. All you need is a touch and your hearing will be restored. I pray that today you walk in peace, patience and kindness toward yourself and others. Remember, we never truly know what someone is going through and a smile can go a long way in someone's life. Always remember, no matter what, share that unique smile with yourself first and then others that cross your path today.

You do what is best for your soul,
because everything else is just noise.
-Mae (Green Leaf)

Make a list of the noises that need to be turned off in your life. Be truthful with yourself. This is between you and God.

_____

_____

_____

_____

_____

_____

_____

_____

_____

_____

_____

_____

_____

_____

_____

_____
Date

Be Present

Good morning! You just woke up in roll call. Will you answer God as, "present" or just be silent? It's time to wake up every morning and answer, "present," because God called you for just a time as this. You have a work to accomplish that was designed just for you and the Holy Ghost Academy is in session. What will you learn from life today or what test will you pass? Everything you need to succeed daily is in you. Don't sit in the back watching your life pass before you. Wake up, get up and be PRESENT. You were not designed to sit in the back of life. I want you to understand that you deserve everything life has to offer. It's time to stop standing back watching life pass you by like you don't deserve everything God has promised you. Now is the time to live like you have a purpose; live like you are someone special and deserve the life you were blessed with. Wake up every day and live your life in the present. Life is too short to not enjoy it and take advantage of why you were given this gift of life and discover your true purpose. Wake up and embrace life like you have something to live for and expect blessings and awesomeness to come your way. The time is now to Be Present and reach for your goals and achieve your purpose. You got this and I believe you can accomplish whatever you put your mind to. Always remember, no matter what, share that unique smile with yourself first and then others that cross your path today.

Wake up everyday and just be Present.

Now is the time to get quiet before God and pray. Write a simple but powerful prayer to just be present in your life everyday. Be truthful with yourself. This is between you and God.

_____

_____

_____

_____

_____

_____

_____

_____

_____

_____

_____

_____

_____

_____

_____

Date

Joy Unspeakable

There is an unspeakable joy ready to arise in your life TODAY! This joy has been laying dormant for way too long and it is ready to come forth. It is time right now to speak to the dry bones of joy and speak life into them so that joy may arise fully in your life. Don't go another day without overflowing in the joy of the Lord. There is no better place I'd rather be in my life than a life overflowing in the fullness of Joy. Every day you are blessed with the gift of life and with that gift comes joy. Satan may come to steal your joy, but you stand sure-footed and let the enemy know that this joy you have the devil can't take it away. Let your joy be so deeply rooted that no storm, situation, or circumstance can uproot your joy. I pray that today and every day will be a joyful moment for you no matter what comes your way. When you fill your life up with God's joy, it starts to overflow onto others. Let your unspeakable joy be contagious so that others will catch that joy and pass it along to others whom they come in contact with. God is saying, "My Joy is undeniable and you cannot run from it; just get in My joyful flow and live." Don't forget to not only overflow your joy onto others, but always remember, no matter what, share that unique smile with yourself first and then others that cross your path today. Be blessed!

*Now is the time to stop holding
back and find the joy in your journey.*

Now is the time to get quiet before God and pray. Write a prayer for God to fill you with an overflowing unspeakable joy. Be truthful with yourself. This is between you and God.

_____

_____

_____

_____

_____

_____

_____

_____

_____

_____

_____

_____

_____

_____

_____

_____

Date

Soulful Self-Care

This pretty much says it all. We must never be afraid of self-care. We must take the time to disconnect and shut off everything and everyone even if it is for 30 minutes. We have to learn to stop and take time to breathe and say, "Right now is my time." How we spend that time to refresh and refocus our life is up to us. Take time to relax, pray and listen. We were blessed with this life for a purpose. Make sure to always take care of yourself. Make it a goal today to do something for yourself. Always remember, no matter what, share that unique smile with yourself first and then others that cross your path today.

Take time for Yourself.

Make a self-care list. This list is all about you and what you can do on your soulful days. Don't be afraid to do something for yourself. Make that list and stick to it and accomplish something for yourself.

_____

_____

_____

_____

_____

_____

_____

_____

_____

_____

_____

_____

_____

_____

_____

_____

_____
Date

On Today

Today is a day to walk out that door into the world ready and confident for whatever is coming your way. You are a daughter of the most High God and nothing is impossible. Everything is possible! You woke up with a gift this morning and that is the breath of life. God saw fit today to wake you up this morning because there is still a greater work to be done here on this earth. Keep your spiritual eyes open and spiritual ears listening to see what your mission is for today. Today ask God what will He have you do today to share His love and encouragement with someone else. As you walk out that door you walk in confidence today, you walk in peace today, you walk in love today, you walk in joy today, you walk in favor today and speak life all day long. TODAY! No matter what comes your way, flash that smile and say to yourself, "I got this because there is a greater One on the inside of me. I shall not be moved and I will walk on to greatness." You are special, you are loved, you are healed, you are free, and there is nothing and no one that can take that from you unless you allow it. So, hold tight to who and whose you are. Don't let go because your life depends on it. Be blessed and carry on!!! Always remember, no matter what, share that unique smile with yourself first and then others that cross your path today.

Today just be blessed & carry on.

Before you walk out that door to start your day take some time to reflect and write down what you desire your day to look like. Pray and ask God to keep you from being moved on Today.

_____

_____

_____

_____

_____

_____

_____

_____

_____

_____

_____

_____

_____

_____

_____

_____

_____
Date

Custom Tailored Just For Me

I deserve this life I have been given, because my life has been custom tailored just for me. I may struggle and wrestle with this customized life because I am trying to comfortably fit in it. I may have tried on many imitations of this life, but it was not the one made just for me. You see, when I slip into the life that has been formed just for me, it will take a minute to get comfortable. The material may fit a little tight at first but, the more I wear this customized life, the more perfectly it will fit. One day it will fit so natural because it should only fit me.

No one can fit my customized life and I will definitely not be able to fit any one else's. I am unique, so every stitch, every seam, every zipper, every button, every bling belongs and was created just for me. As I wear this life it may produce some snags, some rips, maybe even some holes, but that's ok. When this life was customized and created just for me the Tailor knew without a doubt that it wouldn't always remain new. Over time it will get worn and the threads will start to stress under the pulls and pressures of this life.

The Tailor understood that over time it would snag on the trials and decisions that didn't meet the standards of the customized life the Tailor expected. The Tailor knew that it would get ripped and even produce holes because of relationships that weren't meant to be. But the Tailor also knew that the life customized for me could never be destroyed because the Tailor had a special blend of fabric mixed into this customized life of mine. The Tailor added some grace and mercy between the threads of life because He knew it would hold my life together.

The Tailor also ascended my life with love and kindness. This customized life now looks vintage, but that's ok because it will last and last and survive the hands of time just like the Tailor meant for it to be worn. Until one day a whole new customized, perfect outfit will be taken out of the closet where it's been hung just waiting for me to put on and never take off again. Always remember, no matter what, share that unique smile with yourself first and then others that cross your path today.

Journal Time

Make a list of how God has custom tailored your life. Be truthful with yourself. This is between you and God.

_____

_____

_____

_____

_____

_____

_____

_____

_____

_____

_____

_____

_____

_____

Date

Love is Necessary

Love is a powerful main ingredient to life. We must learn to accept and give true love. Love comes in many forms, but make sure to choose true love. In order for us to understand love, we must love ourselves and appreciate and accept who we are. We were created in the image of love, therefore we must overflow in love. Let love guide you in every area of your life. Don't be afraid to love because one of our goals in life is to love ourselves and to let that love overflow to others. One thing I am continuing to learn in my life every day is to trust and accept true love and who I am in Christ Jesus. Don't let your past experiences rob you of true love when it stands right in front of you. Some say love is blind, but when you are a child of the Most High, you are not blinded. You have a clear and precise vision of love. Set a goal today before you walk out that door to your next destination that you'll fill yourself up with love so that it can spill out to others all day long. May you never run out of true love in your life. Always remember, no matter what, share that unique smile with yourself first and then others that cross your path today.

Love is Life,
Love is Kind,
Love is Empathy,
Love is Necessary!

Before you walk out that door to start your day take some time to reflect and write down areas of your life where you need to show more love to yourself and others.

_____

_____

_____

_____

_____

_____

_____

_____

_____

_____

_____

_____

_____

_____

_____
Date

Motivate from Within

Don't allow fear to drive your life, your purpose or your passion. Start to refocus. All you need to do is have faith to believe you can, step out and go for it. Life is too short to sit on the sidelines when you can position yourself on the front-lines of your purpose. We have lingered too long in fear and if there was ever a better time to step out, it is NOW. So, what are you waiting for? Your purpose and destiny are calling and you need to stay focused and go for what you were created for. Live your life to the fullest and enjoy each and every step of the way. Today is a time to be thankful for each and every step you have and are about to take. We've got this together and we can do it in confidence and without fear. Always remember, no matter what, share that unique smile with yourself first and then others that cross your path today.

Stay focused and stay humble in the journey.

Start today by praying a simple prayer and make a list of some goals you would like to accomplish within the next 3 months. Don't overwhelm yourself with goals. Make goals you know you will complete and go for it!

_____

_____

_____

_____

_____

_____

_____

_____

_____

_____

_____

_____

_____

_____

_____

Date

Live Your Life Unapologetically

Don't be afraid to live your life unapologetically! Don't live your life daily tiptoeing through the tulips. It's time to live your life with purpose, by having a made-up mind, and an unwavering faith that can't be explained. We often are too cautious and careful of living worried and scared what others might say or think about us. Let me enlighten you right now and tell you that you aren't living for others. Your life belongs to God and He placed you on this earth for such a time as this. We are to be living examples of light and love because the Christ on the inside of us shines through. Walk confidently everyday in who and whose you are. It's time-out for being intimidated 'cause you don't look, talk, walk, or act like someone else. The Bible says we are not of this world and not to conform to the things of this world. First, know for yourself who you are. This will only take place by humbling yourself, sitting at the feet of Jesus and opening up your heart to begin to let Him show you, you. Take a break from social media - it won't hurt you to stop looking and scrolling. Live your life on purpose and unapologetically how it is meant to be lived. Enjoy where you are right now in life. Always remember, no matter what, share that unique smile with yourself first and then others that cross your path today.

Love the Life you Live!
Why?
Because you deserve it.

If you need to realize how unique you are. Take time to make a list of what make you uniquely you.

_____

_____

_____

_____

_____

_____

_____

_____

_____

_____

_____

_____

_____

_____

Date

Climb Further

Mountains come in our lives to teach us strength, endurance and most of all who we are in Christ Jesus. A solo mountain climber doesn't go looking for the tallest mountain and quickly start climbing. We can learn a great lesson of life from a solo mountain climber. A solo mountain climber has to go face the mountain, study the mountain and consider the weather. She has to determine what route is best to take, estimate how long it will take to conquer the mountain and get to the top. A solo mountain climber has no safety to fall back on if something doesn't go quite as planned. All she has is a focused mindset, strength, endurance, a vision for the end result, and a plan.

We are no different when we are faced with mountains in our lives. You see, some of us are meant to go around mountains while others have no choice but to climb their way to the top and conquer it. Do as the solo mountain climber: face the mountain, pray a plan, let God show you the best route, and climb your way to the top. Pray for strength and endurance to make it. If you get weary on the climb and you slip, just know God's hand is there to catch you and place you just where you need to be in the climb. Have faith to believe you can climb your way out of every situation and when you reach the top, oh what a beautiful view it is! Always remember, everyone is not meant to climb your route of purpose. It won't be easy and it may hurt, but it's necessary to shake off the people and baggage that are slowing you down. You have a certain focus and pace to keep up with on your climb of purpose and you must endure to the end. So, climb lightly on your path and spiritually invest in yourself every day, even if the investment is small. In time, with patience, perseverance and endurance, you will climb further and see a great view. Always remember, no matter what, share that unique smile with yourself first and then others that cross your path today.

The best view comes after the hardest climb.

Now is the time to get quiet before God and pray. Write a prayer to ask God to show you and guide you as you climb further above all circumstances that comes your way. Be truthful with yourself. This is between you and God.

_____

_____

_____

_____

_____

_____

_____

_____

_____

_____

_____

_____

_____

_____

_____

Date

Joy is Necessary

I woke up this morning overflowing with an unspeakable joy. How about you? If you didn't wake up with joy overflowing, I am here to tell you that you have something to be joyful about every day you open your eyes. You see, everyday we wake up God gives us another day to experience Him and see the beauty of His creation. Start waking up with purpose, waking up with expectation, waking up with fullness of joy. Why so downcast oh, my soul? Let joy overtake you like never before for such a time as this. Make this a time of healing the hurts and disappointments that have overtaken your joy. Your joy is still there. It's just buried beneath all the sorrows and cares of this world. It's time now since we are in a season of spring to let that joy spring forth like never before. Not only do you need to experience joy, but everyone you come in contact with needs to experience the joy of the Lord. Joy is contagious, so let's pass on something positive, meaningful and healthy. Something that can last a lifetime. Be contagious with the joy of the Lord and carry on! Have a wonderful, peaceful, joyful, and lovely day in the Lord. Always remember, no matter what, share that unique smile with yourself first and then others that cross your path today.

Walk daily in bubbling joy.

Now is the time to get quiet before God and pray. Write a daily confession to maintain you joy.

_____

_____

_____

_____

_____

_____

_____

_____

_____

_____

_____

_____

_____

_____

_____
Date

Taking Time

Today is a new day to experience God and share who God is with others. Let's make today a day of strength, a day of peace, a day of love. We can do this when we have spent time with God and put our faith and trust in His Word. Today is not a day of fear. Fill your mind, heart and spirit with the Word of God and His many promises He has made to us. He has not left us or forsaken us. God is right here keeping us and upholding us in the palm of His hand. Spend your day being strengthened in Christ Jesus so you can endure this time. Take a little time today to check on others whom the Lord places on your heart. Take this time to pray and praise with those in your home. God created you for a purpose and now is the time to seek that purpose out like never before. He needs each and every one of His children in place for such a time as this. I pray you have a blessed and peaceful day, a day filled with joy and smiles, a day of love overflowing to others, and a day to be a light in the midst of darkness. Today I share my unique smile with everyone of you reading this message and I hope you pass your unique smile on to others as well. Thanks for taking the time to read what flows from my heart to yours. Have a wonderful day and carry on. Always remember, no matter what, share that unique smile with yourself first and then others that cross your path today.

Make today a day of love, peace and joy.

Write a scripture that is dear to your heart at this time and meditate on it all day.

_____

_____

_____

_____

_____

_____

_____

_____

_____

_____

_____

_____

_____

_____

_____

_____

_____

_____

Date

Get Air

I had an eye-opening experience when I took my grand- daughter on an outing. She wanted to jump on the trampoline so I took her to a place that had trampolines. We had so much fun and I got a good workout also. In experiencing this adventure I had a revelation about air. In life all too often we stay grounded without moving into our purpose and toward our destiny. This could be because of fear, lack of finances, no support, who we surround ourselves with and the list could go on and on. We don't even realize our potential, who we are, or where we are going because we are grounded. Life hits us on every side and weighs us down which causes us to be stagnant and stuck. I am here to tell you, my friend, now is the time to get air. Now is the time to leap toward your destiny. By taking that leap means that you are fully trusting God and you have nothing to lose. The revelation God gave me while I was getting air was this: As long as we are grounded we have a false faith towards our destiny; an unsure foundation to move toward, but the good news is, when we take the leap and get air we are directly placed in God's hand and He will carry us toward our destiny. That is when our faith is truly working for our good. God won't drop us. He will elevate us to our purpose and ultimately our destination. Air is constantly moving for a purpose and when we get air and get into the flow of our purpose, we will live a fulfilled life in Jesus Christ. Don't stay grounded and stagnant. Now is the time to get air and move forward to where God purposed you to be. Always remember, no matter what, share that unique smile with yourself first and then others that cross your path today.

Once you rise above where you are the key is to: Get Air and Take Flight.

Take time today to encourage yourself and write a note to self on how proud you are of where you have come in your life and where you are going.

_____

_____

_____

_____

_____

_____

_____

_____

_____

_____

_____

_____

_____

_____

Date

She Believed

She believed past her circumstances
She believed past her finances
She believed past her self
She believed past her storms
She believed past her tears
She believed past her impossibilities
She believed past everything that was
coming against her

She Just Believed!

Where you are in your life you must have a sure foundation that through it all there are better days coming and it won't always be like this. As long as we are living and breathing we will get through, but let each test and trial get easier because we believed. Your inner man has got to be so strong that whatever your outward man is going through: emotionally, physically or spiritually that the inner man will push you through. As you push through make sure to find inner peace to your soul. We have and we must believe that everything concerning us will be ok.

Why? She Just Believed!

She believed
She could so
She did.

Make a list of your accomplishments in your life and if you need to get a piece of paper or journal to write how you achieved those accomplishments.

_____

_____

_____

_____

_____

_____

_____

_____

_____

_____

_____

_____

_____

_____

_____

_____

_____

Date

Just Be Kind

Let's wake up wrapped up and overflowing in kindness. No matter what did or didn't go as planned yesterday or last week, let's look at today as a new start for situations to turn around. You know, when we focus our kindness towards others, our not so great situations become a blur. The Word of God promises that He will take care of His own and He will fight our battles. So, why try and fight a battle we may never win on our own? We need to trust God fully to take care of everything that concerns us and to live our lives as God planned in peace, love and joy in the Holy Ghost. Don't go another day without being kind to yourself first because we can't give what we don't truly have on the inside. Kindness starts on the inside and overflows to the outside onto everyone we speak to or give a smile to. Just be kind and enjoy who you are from the inside out. Let today be at least one goal of kindness and share it with someone. Always remember, no matter what, to share that unique smile with yourself first and then others that cross your path today.

*Be the one who overflows
in kindness towards others.*

Write a kindness letter to yourself straight from the heart. This is between you and God.

_____

_____

_____

_____

_____

_____

_____

_____

_____

_____

_____

_____

_____

_____

Date

Time is on Your Side

Time seems to wait for no one these days. Birthdays and holidays come so quickly now that we barely have time to plan. Time is moving so quickly that it seems the seasons can't even keep up. Fall and spring seem to have faded away and we go from summer to winter. One day we are holding babies; the next, we are looking at our adult children wondering where the time went. With time moving so fast we must take time to make sure that we are in God's time and not our own. We need to use our time wisely and not foolishly. Years, months, day, hours, minutes, seconds are not promised to any of us. God is warning us to use our time wisely because He knows that there are many situations in our lives that distract us from what really matters. Time looks like it is against us until we stop to realize that time is actually on our side, especially once we come to an understanding of our purpose in time. We need to understand that when God created time, He also added balance. So what time is it for you? How are you using your time? We must make sure we are using our time wisely with the vision and purpose God has given to each and every one of us. Get in the flow of God's time and soar to new heights in your life. Have a wonderfully, blessed and awesome day. Always remember, no matter what, share that unique smile with yourself first and then others that cross your path today.

To everything there is a season, a time for
every purpose under heaven:
Ecclesiastes 3:1

Now is the time to get quiet before God and pray. Write a list of where you are now and where you would like to be and give yourself a time line. Be truthful with yourself. This is between you and God.

_____

_____

_____

_____

_____

_____

_____

_____

_____

_____

_____

_____

_____

_____

_____

_____

_____
Date

Inspired to Pray

Prayers of the Heart

Prayer is essential to everyday living. Every day we have another opportunity to see and experience the glory of God. Today is the day to go deeper in your communication with God. God wants prayers from you that will change the atmosphere. He wants to hear the Word of God prayed from your heart that will change you from the inside out. Stop praying surface prayers. It's time to go deeper than ever before when you pray. Pray expecting a change to come. It might not come right then, but it's time to pray expecting God to move on your behalf. God is a God of promise and if He said it, it will come to pass. It won't be in your time frame, but it will come to pass in God's time. Don't fear going deeper in prayer. Instead, embrace every prayer you pray with faith and great expectation. God loves you and is there waiting for you to come to Him in prayer. Have faith that God will hear and give you the desires of your heart. He'll change you from the inside out because you are beautiful from the inside out! Always remember, no matter what, to share that unique smile with yourself first and then others that cross your path today.

Call to me, and I will answer you, and show you great and mighty things, which you do not know.
Jeremiah 33:3

Make a list of each area that needs God's attention. Be truthful with yourself. This is between you and God.

_____

_____

_____

_____

_____

_____

_____

_____

_____

_____

_____

_____

_____

_____

_____

_____

_____
Date

Develop A Passion for Prayer

We cannot live on this earth day in and day out without prayer in our lives. Prayer is another key ingredient for life. Prayer is our lifeline, our direct line, our main communication with our Father. Prayer is not always easy and prayer takes practice. Why? Because it is necessary. Just like we exercise for our health; we must pray for our lives. Prayer can have us so in-tune with God that it is like a natural conversation. There is no need to get discouraged in your prayer life because the Bible is full of examples about how we should pray, when we should pray and where we can pray. A key to prayer is not to wait until all hell breaks loose in your life to start praying. Prayer starts when everything is going well and nothing is hitting you on all sides. Your prayer life doesn't have to mimic someone else's prayer life. Your prayer life is like your thumbprint - specific to who you are. You don't have to pray for hours to get God's attention. The key to prayer is a pure heart. Start today by offering up to God a sincere prayer from the heart. Be consistent with your prayer life and expect a life full of peace. Always remember, no matter what, share that unique smile with yourself first and then others that cross your path today.

In this manner, therefore, pray:
Our Father in heaven, Hallowed be Your name.
Your kingdom come. Your will be done On earth
as it is in heaven. Give us this day our daily bread.
And forgive us our debts, As we forgive our debtors.
And do not lead us into temptation, But deliver us
from the evil one. For Yours is the kingdom and
the power and the glory forever. Amen.
Matthew 6:9-13

Now is the time to get quiet before God and pray. Write some prayer goals you would like to achieve in the next 30 days.

_____

_____

_____

_____

_____

_____

_____

_____

_____

_____

_____

_____

_____

_____

_____

Date

In the Still Small Voice

It is exciting to know that even through all of the noise and confusion, God can still be heard loud and clear. Don't be discouraged because God is speaking louder than we know. All we need to do is tune our ears to listen to that still small voice and be obedient to the instruction He is giving us. There is peace in the middle of a storm. Get in the center of God's will for your life and listen to that still small voice. May today be a day of peace, hope, faith, love, and joy in Jesus Christ. Pray today that God continues to speak to those that will take the time to listen. Always remember, no matter what, share that unique smile with yourself first and then others that cross your path today.

"But whoever listens to me will dwell safely,
And will be secure, without fear of evil.
Proverbs 1:33

Now is the time to get quiet before God and pray. Write a prayer to God for discipline to hear for that still small voice and allow Him to commune with you. Be truthful with yourself. This is between you and God.

_____

_____

_____

_____

_____

_____

_____

_____

_____

_____

_____

_____

_____

_____

Date

I Stand at the Door and Knock

God woke me up this morning to ask, "Have you put Me first?" I am returning you back to your first love. Back to our first encounter together when we first met. Even though you strayed far from Me, I never left you. I have always stood at the door and knocked and still to this day, I continue to knock. The question is, "will you answer and return unto Me?" Don't let another day, a moment or a second pass by that you won't answer. I am waiting for you, My child, with open arms to answer My call. My summoning you is not loud and boisterous as thunder to get your attention. My coming after you is a gentle small whisper, the cool breeze on a nice spring morning and the birds chirping at daybreak. Don't ignore the still small voice. I am as the Shepherd coming after the one that has gone astray. It's time to put Me back first in your life, back to your first love. Look to Me and I will give you peace in the midst of everything going on around you. Refocus your life in Me and don't be distracted by the noise. Look up to the hills from where your help comes from. Don't be afraid of man and the news going forth. Get in My Word and abide in Me; that is where your truth will come from. With Me there is clarity and confusion cannot stay. Be the light in the midst of darkness and shine bright. We have a job to do and the time is now that the work begins. Strengthen your mind, body and spirit in My Word and stay strong through the midst of everything going on and what's about to happen. Don't give up because I will be with you always. Press your way through no matter what. May peace, joy and love abide with you today. Watch My mercy and grace follow you where the soles of your feet tread. Take your rest and know, My child, that you are in the palm of My hand. Always remember, no matter what, share that unique smile with yourself first and then others that cross your path today.

Behold, I stand at the door and knock. If anyone hears My voice and opens the door, I will come in to him and dine with him, and he with Me. Revelation 3:20

Now is the time to get quiet before God and pray. Start today by praying a simple prayer and asking God to remain the center of your life. Be truthful with yourself. This is between you and God.

_____

_____

_____

_____

_____

_____

_____

_____

_____

_____

_____

_____

_____

_____

_____

Date

What is Your Response?

Yesterday, I watched my cousin on Facebook make homemade biscuits and my focus was on those "Amen-praise biscuits." I called them that because he played a song that got my full attention. I had heard the song plenty of times, but this time I heard it differently. When I got up this morning that song was still ringing in my spirit. I played it and as I read the lyrics, this is what God revealed: How many of us know God has already spoken and our full response should be Amen? God has spoken about your current situation. He has spoken about what is going on globally. He has spoken about that wayward family member. He has spoken about your finances. God has spoken about everything concerning your life. The question is, "What should our response be?" We should have a unified voice at this moment in time of "Amen" because God has spoken, and it is already done. Our answers we are seeking are already answered. The healing of our bodies is already whole and complete. Your future has already been laid out just for you.

God is saying,"Do not fear, My child, for I am with you. I am right beside you giving you the peace and comfort you need for such a time as this. Find encouragement during this time and seek Me daily because everything you need I have spoken. And no matter what the situation looks like, your concerns have already been answered. Now step forth and receive peace, peace deep down to carry you through day to day. I left you with a Comforter years ago and that same Comforter still remains here today. Wake up every day with an Amen-spirit because My words will not fail. Just know that what is going on right now in your life, and globally, I am working behind the scenes. All I need you to do is trust Me with your whole heart, mind and spirit. Everything you need I have placed inside you when I formed you in your mother's womb and it still remains. Now is the time to wake up who you are in Christ Jesus and stop fearing who I created you to be. Be comforted knowing that I have spoken, and your response should be AMEN!" Always remember, no matter what, share that unique smile with yourself first and then others that cross your path today.

Now is the time to get quiet before God and pray. Write a confession for God to give you the correct response in every daily situation. Be truthful with yourself. This is between you and God.

_____

_____

_____

_____

_____

_____

_____

_____

_____

_____

_____

_____

_____

_____

_____

_____

_____
Date

Have a Little Talk with Jesus

Do you realize the same way you start your day is the same way you should end your day? Speaking and listening to God. It is a gift from God every morning you open your eyes, so don't take it for granted. God should be the first one on your mind. Not reaching for that cell phone or TV remote. No, you should be talking with God and letting Him talk to you. You may need a good strategy for the day because God knows what you are about to face before your feet even hit the floor. Stop sleeping your time away from God. Get disciplined in your life to commune with God daily.

He misses us dearly and longs for those prayers and talks from our hearts. If we start our day off with God then He walks and talks with us all day long. Let's not miss another opportunity to be pleasing to our Heavenly Father. He is sitting right here waiting for us to open our hearts and mouths and talk to Him. Other times He is just waiting for us to sit at His feet while He talks to us. We don't always have to be the one talking! Sometimes we talk too much. We need to hush and listen to God. In this time we need to learn to be at peace alone with God and get to know Him for ourselves. And while we're at it, we'll get to truly know ourselves. Always remember, no matter what, share that unique smile with yourself first and then others that cross your path today.

Rejoice always, pray without ceasing, in everything give thanks: for this is the will of God in Christ Jesus for you.
1 Thessalonians 5:16-18

Now is the time to get quiet before God and pray. Now is the time to sincerely talk to Your Heavenly Father. Open up your heart. Be truthful with yourself. This is between you and God.

_____

_____

_____

_____

_____

_____

_____

_____

_____

_____

_____

_____

_____

_____

_____

_____

_____
Date

Never Stop Praying

Oh, what a beautiful day to Magnify the Lord! Will you magnify the Lord with me? Let's exalt His name together. I ran across a prayer challenge on Facebook which said to pray 5 days for 5 minutes and I wanted to share it with you. We need to pray, pray, pray and pray some more. This is a time of getting your prayer life in order. They say when this pandemic is over that it won't be normal again, but my question to you is, "What is normal?" Were our lives before this pandemic normal? Was your busy life normal? Was that job you went to every day normal? Was that bank account normal? Was your family time normal? Ask yourself, "what was normal?"

Sometimes I will look up a word just to understand. I've helped you and looked up the word, "normal." Normal means conforming to a type, standard, or regular pattern. After reading this, I have come to realize that our lives weren't normal after all because of the patterns we lived every day. We need to go beyond normal or our definition of normal and get a Heavenly normal. What does that look like? One simple but powerful word: PRAY. You want to move mountains in your life? Pray. You want to have peace and joy in your life? Pray. You want to embrace more of Jesus? Pray. You want to understand your purpose? Pray. You want to overcome fear and doubt? Pray. You want a healing in your body? Pray. I will let you add to this list because only you and God know where you are in your life. I am just here to encourage you. When we pray the atmosphere shifts and it is a pleasing sound to God. Don't slip up at this time in your life and not pray. Get up, look up and pray because God is waiting to hear from you. Now, my question to you is, "what are you waiting for?" PRAY!!! Always remember, no matter what, share that unique smile with yourself first and then others that cross your path today.

Praying Consistently means hearing from God consistently.

Now is the time to get quiet before God and pray. Write a prayer asking the Lord to develop a consistent prayer life.

_____

_____

_____

_____

_____

_____

_____

_____

_____

_____

_____

_____

_____

_____

_____

_____

_____

_____

Date

Inspired Confessions

Speak Life

Always remember that even in your brokenness, you can find comfort and healing. The scripture says: *Let your conduct be without covetousness; be content with such things as you have. For He Himself has said, "I will never leave you nor forsake you." Hebrews 13:5.* It is time to take God at His Word and speak life. If God is here for us, then who can be against us? We have the power in our tongue to speak life over our lives and others. Stop speaking the opposite of what God has promised in His Word. God promises us life. He breathed into us the breath of life. We need to treasure the gift of life and live it according to God's Word. It's time to start pressing through the brokenness in prayer to the One who can piece you back together and has your best interest at hand. Seek God daily for guidance and instruction in your life's journey of healing. Being broken is a good thing because your strength can be restored. When God reaches down and picks up the pieces of your life — only the pieces He deems good and very good — He can piece you back together to wholeness. It's exciting to know that the pieces God can't use He'll replace with perfect pieces He designed just for You. You are unique and beautiful from the inside out. Be encouraged today just knowing that you have everything you need on the inside of you to enjoy the life you're blessed with. Live your life in confidence knowing that you are healed, whole and complete in Christ Jesus. Always remember, no matter what, to share that unique smile with yourself first and then others that cross your path today.

Dear Lord,
When I fall, catch me.
When I'm sad, comfort me.
When I cry, dry my tears.
When I'm broken, make me whole again.
In Jesus Name, Amen.

Now is the time to make a list of life sustaining confessions. Write down confessions you can speak over your life daily that brings life to your spirit. You must learn how to encourage yourself and speak over yourself daily. Enjoy the life you were blessed with and live.

_____

_____

_____

_____

_____

_____

_____

_____

_____

_____

_____

_____

_____

_____

_____
Date

Living a Life: Free, Healed & Complete

One thing in my life I have become in tune with is when the Lord speaks. We must get to a place in our lives to recognize when something's brought before us more than once, it may be something the Lord is trying to tell or show us. Don't become so busy and self-absorbed with your life that you miss the Lord speaking. Understand that what you are consumed with in your life that you think is overtaking you could be the Lord easing you out of that situation through a still small voice. Don't stay in a situation longer than you are supposed to because it will profit you nothing to remain. We must learn to be sensitive to the Holy Spirit. It is time to do as the Word says and move into a season of healing and restoration. In order to get through this season in our lives we must pray and seek His face and turn from those areas that the Lord has already shown us that are toxic. Don't be stubborn and hold on to toxic people, toxic situations, toxic mindsets, or toxic speaking. We must let go in order to fulfill our purpose designed just for us. Once we let go of the toxic areas in our lives then we will be forgiven of the sin and healed. Don't you want to enter into your destiny and promises with a life free, whole and complete in Christ Jesus? Well, what are you waiting for? Let's take this step together, support one another, encourage one another, and most of all PRAY!!! No matter what you are going through at this very moment, always remember nothing is too hard for God. Get up from where you are, raise your hands as high as you can to the heavens and ask God to heal your land, create in you a clean heart, give you a renewed mindset, and the strength to get through the situation you are facing. One thing to know is you will never be alone. Just stay sensitive to the Holy Spirit and let Him lead and guide you every step of the way. Always remember, no matter what, to share that unique smile with yourself first and then others that cross your path today.

Live your life to the fullest.
Your breakthrough is on the other side of fear.

Now is the time to write a heartfelt sincere prayer to God. Talk to God about your life and where you desire to be. Write down what He is speaking to you. Be truthful with yourself. This is between you and God.

_____

_____

_____

_____

_____

_____

_____

_____

_____

_____

_____

_____

_____

Date

Adjust that Crown

Life is precious and we need to enjoy it to the fullest. We can live our best life now by doing simple things in life, such as sharing a smile or a kind word because we all need encouragement.

You are somebody and you can do anything you put your mind to. How do I know this? Because my Heavenly Father promised it to me in His Word:

> *I can do all things through Christ who strengthens me.*
> *Philippians 4:13*

You have the same promise that I have. No one is better than another. We all are on an even playing field in God's eyes. The only difference between us is that we are in different places in our lives. One thing for sure that we have in common is that we all should have heaven in our view. Our destination is the same. We are on different paths and purposes to get us there. So stop tearing yourself down and those around you because our Father has promised us just the same. Don't let fear overtake you, but move out to do something that scares you and takes you out of your comfort zone. It's time to fix your crown, stand proud and walk with confidence because you are special and you are somebody.

I am happy to know that you are my sister! We are standing together and walking in our purpose. Don't doubt or fear who you are. You, yes you, are on this earth for a purpose. If you are unsure of your purpose, spend some quiet time and seek who you are and what your purpose is. Don't compare yourself to another person. We are all unique individuals on different paths of life with a common goal and hopefully that goal is to live your most enjoyable life now. Enjoy this day and your life in full bloom and encourage another woman today! Always remember, no matter what, share that unique smile with yourself first and then others that cross your path today.

Always wear your invisible crown.

Now is the time to get quiet before God and let Him reveal to you your purpose and plan He has for You. Now, He wont give it to you all at once, but what He does reveal to you make a list write it down and add to it as He reveals His purpose in your life.

_____

_____

_____

_____

_____

_____

_____

_____

_____

_____

_____

_____

_____

_____

_____

Date

You are Strong

When early mornings or life in general has you not feeling your best self, but you still have to share a "Good Morning" ('cause that's who you are), get up, go straight to the mirror and give yourself a great big smile. You see, a smile can be the cure for what has you worried, stressed, depressed. So just remember, we all could use a smile.

Besides, that smile looks good on you, my friend! Every day is not going to be a tiptoe through the tulips. Some days are going to be harder than others. Do not beat yourself up for your difficult days, because we are not perfect. Just remember not to take your actions out on someone else. Ask God to show you how to get through the day and to strengthen your spirit so that you can have peace. Storms come and go in our lives, some come with a warning and others pop up instantly with no warning at all. As long as you start every day in Christ Jesus, no matter how your day goes, you will be able to walk through those storms and keep your eyes on Christ Jesus. He is right there telling you in that still small voice:

Be of good cheer!
It is I; do not be afraid. Matthew 14:27

Do not allow your storms to cause you to lose faith. Stop looking at the storms and look to the peace in the storms. While your life may be tossing to and fro, remember Jesus is in the back of your boat asleep. As long as Jesus is in your life, you have nothing to fear or doubt. Only in His timing will He speak to the storms in your life and cause them to cease. Always know storms in our lives come to make us stronger and not weaker. Take the time to learn all you can in the storms of your life. You will make it through to the other side. Just keep Jesus in your life and pray without ceasing when you are being tossed to and fro. Remember to smile through the storm and be at peace 'cause better is in store for you. Always remember, no matter what, share that unique smile with yourself first and then others that cross your path today.

Now is the time to get quiet before God and pray. Write a prayer for God to strengthen you daily.

_____

_____

_____

_____

_____

_____

_____

_____

_____

_____

_____

_____

_____

_____

Date

Be Grateful, Daily

No matter what happened yesterday, today is a new day and we need to start it with a grateful heart. You see, the Lord didn't have to awaken us this morning, but He did because He knows we still have work to do. Don't be discouraged, stressed or down because yesterday didn't go quite as planned. Maybe it was for our best interest and protection to be that way. Today is a new day to take on a whole new perspective and see what our Heavenly Father has in store. Today is a day that we have a clean slate to listen for instructions on how to make this day awesome. We live by faith and not by sight, so we should have an expectation of a peaceful day no matter what is coming our way. If you have gotten up and started your day with the Lord, you have a confidence to say, "my today will be even better than my yesterday." Let's get up, get out and touch someone else with the overflowing joy and peace we have. Always remember, no matter what, share that unique smile with yourself first and then others that cross your path today.

Make a joyful shout to the Lord, all you lands!
Serve the Lord with gladness; Come before
His presence with singing. Know that the Lord,
He is God; It is He who has made us, and not we
ourselves; We are His people and the sheep of His
pasture. Enter into His gates with thanksgiving,
And into His courts with praise. Be thankful to Him,
and bless His name. For the Lord is good; His mercy is
everlasting, And His truth endures to all generations.
Psalm 100:1-5

Now is the time to get quiet before God and pray. Write a prayer asking God to help you start each day with a grateful heart. Be truthful with yourself. This is between you and God.

_____

_____

_____

_____

_____

_____

_____

_____

_____

_____

_____

_____

_____

_____

Date

Have Great Faith

It's time for us to step into the promises God has prepared for us. It's time for us to push fear aside and away from our mindset. If God brought us to it, He can definitely bring us through it. He sees and knows all, so why do we fear what we cannot see? It's time to trust God in each and every step we make on our life's journey. If we pray and spend time with God on a daily basis then there's nothing to fear when we can't see what's around the corner. Most of the time we don't need to see what is ahead because we might just detour because we don't believe we can handle it. We must build up our most holy faith and go full steam ahead because God has us in the palm of His hand and He will never give us more than we can bear. Don't be afraid to take the first step. I guarantee, the finish line is more than we can imagine. Let's take the first step together and watch what happens in our lives. Let's expect greatness in our lives and the ability to overcome the bumps in the road because we know who and whose we are. Always remember, no matter what, share that unique smile with yourself first and then others that cross your path today.

Faith is taking that first step into the promises of God even if you can't see the path.

Now is the time to get quiet before God and pray. Write a prayer that your faith be increased daily.

_____

_____

_____

_____

_____

_____

_____

_____

_____

_____

_____

_____

_____

_____

_____
Date

Smile Daily

No matter what has been thrown at you in the last 24 to 48 hrs., always remember, it was only a test. If we have prepared in prayer, studied and spent time with God, then we have got nothing to do but smile through it all. Don't fail the test before it even gets started by letting our minds go the wrong way or our emotions derail us. As long as we stay ready and prepared for a test, then we can smile right on through it and never miss a beat. Remember, the wrong reaction when the test is placed in front of us can lead to a failing grade. If we're not ready, let's get ready by prayer and time in the Word. Let's go on and pass this test because I assure you if you fail, a make-up test is on the way. If we pass, just know that the quiz is around the corner to make sure we still understand and will not be moved by the wrong reaction. We've got nothing else to do but smile. Enjoy your journey of life and smile with every step. May you have a peaceful, joyful and productive day. Always remember, no matter what, share that unique smile with yourself first and then others that cross your path today.

Wear your smile daily it looks good on you.

Make a list of some things or situations that make you smile. How can you smile more in your life?

_____

_____

_____

_____

_____

_____

_____

_____

_____

_____

_____

_____

_____

_____

_____

_____

_____

Date

Speak Over Yourself

The title above should speak volumes to each and every one of us that reads it. We spend too much of our lives doubting ourselves, our abilities, our gifts, our happiness, and doubting who we are. It's time to take back "you" and tell yourself every day when you wake up, who you are, what gifts you have, what you can accomplish in your life, even to love yourself just the way you are. Yes, we all have areas in our life for improvement, but why not start first building up that confidence of who you were created to be? Speak positive words over your life, smile at yourself, hug yourself. When you accomplish this, you'll have mastered a goal of confidence, self-love and acceptance. Don't be afraid of who you are! Embrace every fiber of your being and live life to the fullest.

**The way you
speak to yourself
matters the most.**

Starting today, learn to speak over yourself. Only you know what you truly desire. We all could probably use a little more joy today. So why not take the first step and speak joy within and over your life. May you overflow with so much joy today that it spills over onto someone else. We must change our mindsets and start to speak over our lives what we desire for our lives. Make it a goal today to share a contagious joy so that everyone we pass or come in contact with will catch that overflowing joy. Always remember, no matter what, share that unique smile with yourself first and then others that cross your path today.

*Watch what comes
out of your mouth because
your words have power.*

Yes, you have already written confessions over yourself. Now make another list of confessions to encourage your life daily. You must speak over yourself to encourage yourself.

_____

_____

_____

_____

_____

_____

_____

_____

_____

_____

_____

_____

_____

_____

_____

_____

_____

Date

The Lord is My Shepherd

I have to have a firm confidence that the Lord is actually my Shepherd leading and guiding me in the way everlasting. Do I stray? But of course, but one thing I do know is how to get back to the Shepherd. Sometimes He has to come and bring me back 'cause I get so far out there, and it is for my safety to stay close to the Shepherd. Life is real, struggle is real, but it's all part of God's plan for my life. I am not the focus of my life. What I go through is not the focus of my life. I am not placed on this earth for my benefit and what I can gain or obtain. God's plan is so much more than the plan I think I have and what direction I think I ought to be going in. God didn't place me on this earth with no rhyme or reason, nor instruction or direction. God's timing is perfect and without flaws. Whenever I was born it was for just a time as this. God didn't want me to be born at the beginning of time. He wanted me born on a specific day at a specific time. Everything is happening for a reason on a specific day at a specific time. Don't think it strange when situations come about. God is either preparing you, teaching you or leading you. It is time for us to know and understand what season and stage of life we're in at this hour. Always remember, no matter what, share that unique smile with yourself first and then others that cross your path today.

The Lord is my shepherd; I shall not want.
Psalm 23:1

Now is the time to get quiet before God and pray. Write a prayer asking God to guide you every day on your life's journey.

_____

_____

_____

_____

_____

_____

_____

_____

_____

_____

_____

_____

_____

_____

_____

Date

Inspired to Press

Don't Give Up

Don't give up just 'cause life is beating you down. All too often we give up on life, on an idea, on a person all because it gets too hard. Well, I am here to tell you, this life we walk is not easy and sometimes our decisions and actions cause us to climb the backside of the mountain when God told us to walk around the mountain. Our obedience to God daily will make for an easier life if we would just listen to God.

Now one thing for sure is that this life we walk every day is not easy, but it is not impossible. Keep your head above the mess and the struggles and you will get through. Ask God to give you feet like hinds' feet to leap over your struggles and the mess you encounter. Our storms are here to make us stronger and wiser.

Remember, don't just go through the storms. Make sure you learn something in the storms so that you may encourage not only yourself, but others that may be going through. Live your life to encourage others. Life is precious and meant to be lived in peace, love and joy. We were not given this life to be centered around just us. Stop being selfish with your life and "what about me" attitude. This might sting a little, but it's not about you. We are on this earth to carry out God's plan and He deserves all the glory, not us. Stay focused today on your purpose and make sure no matter what you are going through, don't wear it on your face. Always share a smile and have hope to know that it is getting better no matter what. Realize also that it's not always what you see. Start to see in the Spirit and ask God to focus your spiritual vision so that You can see only what He desires you to see. When we see by the spirit we won't give up on any areas of our lives. Always remember, no matter what, share that unique smile with yourself first and then others that cross your path today.

Trust the process every day no matter what the situation looks like and never give up.

Now is the time to get quiet before God and pray. Write a prayer that God would give you a new perspective, strength and plan to overcome in your situation.

_____

_____

_____

_____

_____

_____

_____

_____

_____

_____

_____

_____

_____

_____

_____

_____

_____

Date

Focused Mindset

If you haven't heard it lately, your mindset determines how we will live our lives daily. When our mindset is toxic, our lives are toxic. We must make a daily confession that our thoughts are positive, peaceful and we live a life with positive vibes. Now this is not easy when we live in a world of chaos, but it's not impossible. Just like we have to discipline our lives to be healthy by exercising our bodies, we must discipline our minds to be focused by exercising peaceful thoughts on a daily basis. Don't get discouraged because this will take time, If we start by casting down every negative thought, we will start to change our mindset, one peaceful thought at a time. Stand on the scripture that says:

Casting down arguments and every high thing that exalts itself against the knowledge of God, bringing every thought into captivity to the obedience of Christ, 2 Corinthians 10:5

Casting down thoughts is more than an everyday process. It's an every second process. Our minds are constantly thinking. This is why we need to fill our hearts and minds with the Word of God so that His word will flow like rivers of living water out of our hearts and minds. Discipline your mind to be in Christ. Let's start today making a strong effort to think differently and change our mindset for the better so that we live a fulfilling life. Always remember, no matter what, to share that unique smile with yourself first and then others that cross your path today.

Everyday focus on what's positive and peaceful.

Now is the time to get quiet before God and pray. Allow God to show you what it will take to focus your mind. Make a list of what He speaks to you about your mindset.

_____

_____

_____

_____

_____

_____

_____

_____

_____

_____

_____

_____

_____

_____

_____

_____

_____

Date

You Got This

My, how time is flying by. I have asked the Lord to overflow you with His love and kindness this day and that His will be done your life. We all can never get enough of God's love and we all can use some extra kindness in our lives. Let's make it a goal this day to encourage and be kind to someone. You see, we can't live a fulfilled life holding a person hostage in our hearts and minds. We need to learn to forgive and let go. You see, some people were not destined to be in your life forever. Some people in your life were in your life only for a season and now the season has changed and it's time to say goodbye and let them go. Some people are placed in our lives for a test. We need to learn how to recognize the test and pass it with flying colors and keep it moving. Stop holding on to someone because you could be keeping them from walking in their destiny and the time has come for you to part ways. Learn to forgive those who have wronged you and pray for those who have caused you pain. But one thing's for sure, we must look in the mirror no matter how hard it may be and repent for any wrongs we have created against another. We must forgive ourselves for even having a wrong mindset toward ourselves. It's time to be honest with ourselves no matter how much it hurts and get it right before God. Go through the pain because it is a whole lot better on the other side. Get in the boat of your life with Christ and get to the other side 'cause your life will be a whole lot better. None of us are perfect and we all have flaws in our lives. Be truthful with yourself and start working on you. Don't go through another year carrying aught against another into the next year. Always remember, how you end is how you enter. Ask God to show you, *you* and deal with what you need to deal with. I hope that today will be an awesome day for you. Always remember, no matter what, to share that unique smile with yourself first and then others that cross your path today.

Just bask in the overflow of God's promises cause you definitely got this.

Now is the time to get quiet before God and let Him reveal to you who you are holding hostage in your heart. Ask God to forgive you and change your heart. Be truthful with yourself. This is between you and God.

_____

_____

_____

_____

_____

_____

_____

_____

_____

_____

_____

_____

_____

_____

Date

It's Time to Get in the Game

My prayer today is that you are encouraged right where you are in life. It's time to stop being surface Christians and go deeper. We have passed the milk stage of life and the expiration date is way past "good," so now is the time to experience the meat stage of life.

Get up, stand up, get off the side line, stop being an observer and get on the field of life and get in position, get in place and get in the purpose God has called you to. No one can play your position but you and if you are not in place, the plays won't work. Don't stay out of position because eventually you will be replaced with the second string. Stop hesitating because God is calling the very play where you are key to His plan. Recess is over. We have run out of time outs; there aren't any more left. Class is in session. We have learned and soaked up spiritual knowledge long enough. Now is the time to live a life of practical living to walk in what you have learned in the spiritual classroom.

In football, there is a plan to win and a strategy developed to beat the opponent. God has just called the next play: we have come out of the locker room, we are standing on God's Kingdom Field, we have memorized the plays and they are in us to run. You see, we are facing our opponent and we look outnumbered, but little does he know… our size does not determine our Victory! It's what he can't see on the inside of us that's bigger than him. You see, we have been coached by the best Head Coach we could ever ask for and when our opponent comes at us, we will always win and have victory cause our Coach has taught us the trick plays of our opponent. As long as you follow the play book (Bible) you will not lose. Have a blessed, awesome and victorious day. Always remember, no matter what, share that unique smile with yourself first and then others that cross your path today.

Don't stay on the sideline make it a priority today to get in the game and win.

Now is the time to get quiet before God and pray. It's time to write a game plan for your life and ask God to keep you focused on the plays. So that you may come out victorious.

_____

_____

_____

_____

_____

_____

_____

_____

_____

_____

_____

_____

_____

_____

Date

Keep Going

When you feel like you are being passed over and everyone around you seems to be winning, DO NOT get discouraged because it's not your turn. God is saying, "Wait patiently. Just go and do as I have instructed. I am watching you and I am right there beside you. Trust me 'cause I got you." God is instructing us to build our endurance for the long journey ahead. Strengthen yourself and especially the inner woman for the battle ahead. You see, every level of your journey requires different parts of yourself to continue on this journey. God knows that the very next level of your journey is going to require more of you. God needs you ready and familiar with the plan he has placed before you. The obstacle course of life God has designed for you requires all of you. You can take this journey and you can enjoy your life. But always remember, God has not forgotten about you on this journey of life. He is right beside you coaching you every step of the way. He is right beside you when you need a water break and sending you to just the right scripture to quench that thirst to continue on to the next stretch of your journey. Don't give up, don't give in 'cause your journey is well underway and God needs you to finish. Always remember, no matter what, share that unique smile with yourself first and then others that cross your path today.

Giving up is not an option because great things take time and it's all in your season.

144

Spend time in prayer and listening to what God has to say that can get you closer to the purpose He designed you for. Make a to do list that will get you one step closer to your purpose.

_____

_____

_____

_____

_____

_____

_____

_____

_____

_____

_____

_____

_____

_____

_____

Date

It's Time to Go

It's time to see beyond where you are.
It's time to stop fearing and GO.
Not matter the distance, no matter the time,
no matter what you or others think.
It's time to move beyond your thoughts,
beyond your box, beyond the wall.
There is no limit to where you are about to GO.
Live your life on GO!
Don't stop for anyone... not even yourself.
Set your life on cruise control and GO.
God says, "There's more for you and what
I need you to do."
Get out of park, move away from idle, and GO.
Whatever is holding you back
- time, people, your thoughts, your fears -
whatever it may be,
let it go and GO!
Time waits for no one and My time is different than man.
So, GO, My child, roll into My flow and GO,
'cause the time is NOW.
In My GO, the flow of restoration is coming:
family is restored, life is restored,
finances are restored, and health is restored.
Don't look to see who is doing or not doing what.
You walk to your own drumbeat;
the beat I have designed just for you.
Get into the unique flow I have prepared just for
you and GO.
Because there is a great work to be done,
and the time is NOW, SO, GO!!!

Now is the time to get quiet before God and pray. Write a confession for God to give you a heart of going beyond where you are. Be truthful with yourself. This is between you and God.

_____

_____

_____

_____

_____

_____

_____

_____

_____

_____

_____

_____

_____

_____

_____

_____

_____

_____

_____

_____

Date

Rise Above

Just a little Wisdom for your day. We must learn to rise above the distractions in our lives. When life hits us hard as it sometimes will, we must learn to rise above. We deserve to live our lives daily in peace and joy. Don't lose focus of who you are and your purpose for living. Take a stand today for **you** and everything else will fall in place. Keep moving and don't stop for anything or anyone. Staying focused and being disciplined in your prayer life and spending time with the Lord is what you need to soar above every issue and distraction that comes your way. Learn how to take flight in your life and rise above so that you stay the course that was specifically designed for you. It's easier to take flight with the wind, but sometimes to get through the storm we need to use our situations to elevate us above and not beneath. Always remember, you have an awesome Father that keeps you in the palm of His hand and will not let you fall. Stay the course and make today a day of soaring to new heights in your life. Always remember, no matter what, share that unique smile with yourself first and then others that cross your path today.

When everything is coming against you
all at once make sure to take wind
and rise above the noise.

Now is the time to get quiet before God and pray. Write a simple but powerful prayer to rise above every distraction in your life. Be truthful with yourself. This is between you and God.

_____

_____

_____

_____

_____

_____

_____

_____

_____

_____

_____

_____

_____

_____

_____

_____

_____

_____

Date

You Can Do More

Trusting yourself is one key to enjoying your life. We need to truly understand who we are, whose we are and how to be honest with ourselves. It is time for an inner reflection of our true selves. We can do so much more in our lives than we even give ourselves credit for. Start today by changing your mindset about yourself and build up your confidence to trust yourself. We are daughters of the Most High and in Him we should have complete confidence. Other people's opinion of you don't matter. What matters is that you trust yourself enough to believe that you can have a wonderful life. I am not talking about money, success, work, etc. I am talking about the life you have been blessed to live daily. God has created you for such a time as this. Now go, seek God to understand your purpose He has created you for this moment in time. Know that you can have the best life right now and go for it. Life is too short to miss the best opportunities because of unhealthy mindsets, discouragements and distractions. Get up, show up, dress up and get your life back and enjoy every breath you breathe. Always remember to keep a humble spirit in knowing who you are and who you were created to be. Once God shows you who you are, grab hold of it and don't let go. People and situations will always be there to try and snatch who you are. Guard your identity and protect who and whose you are. The enemy will be there to steal, kill and destroy, but just know you have the power of the Holy Spirit to command the enemy to flee. Do not fear who you are in Christ Jesus because He has given you a promise and a right to be His child. He is our Abba Father. Now go live like a child of God daily. Remain and always stay humble in the journey! Always remember, no matter what, share that unique smile with yourself first and then others that cross your path today.

You can do more than you think.

Now is the time to get quiet before God and pray. Study the Word of God and make a list of who God has promised you to be. Pray this list daily in your life and be open for God to make changes where needed. Be truthful with yourself. This is between you and God.

_____

_____

_____

_____

_____

_____

_____

_____

_____

_____

_____

_____

_____

_____

_____
Date

Waves of Change

Our lives go through many changes the longer we are here on this earth. Some of those changes are our life's true direction, but we must stop and be observant of what our waves of change are trying to show us. Don't be so busy in your life that you don't stop and take notice of where your life's changes are leading. Always remember, change is a good thing and we must have the courage to embrace that change because we never know what is on the other side of those waves. Don't fear change, but face it head on with confidence… even if you can't see what's ahead of you. You got this, so go forth knowing that your life is a gift and live every day to the fullest. Always remember, no matter what, share that unique smile with yourself first and then others that cross your path today.

*In the waves of change
we find our true direction!*

It's time to make a list of the waves of change in your life. Ask God to show you what changes He is trying to make in your life. Embrace and pray about the changes coming about in your life and flow with God. Be truthful with yourself. This is between you and God.

_____

_____

_____

_____

_____

_____

_____

_____

_____

_____

_____

_____

_____

_____

Date

Seasons for a Reason

As I woke up this morning, I thought about it being October and I had to decide right then that this was going to be the best month of the year for me. In the past, October has been a month of struggles in my life, but this go around, I have chosen a different mindset. Just like this month, all other months and days were created by God. As I've always enjoyed spring, this month will be no different because I have God on my side. You see, God gave us seasons for a reason in our lives. We must learn to embrace each and every season as a gift from God. Some seasons are easier than others and every season produces change. Don't fear or run from the season you are in, because there is a time for everything under the heavens. We are upon the season of fall so this means there will be some falling away. The trees don't stay green forever. They must lose their leaves to produce fresh, renewed leaves in the spring. We also produce throughout the year. What we don't need or think we need, God prunes it, cuts it away and then it falls off of us. Maybe in your life you aren't in your fall season, but just remember seasons are there to mature and grow us and move us closer to God. Stay in constant prayer with the Father so in your season you will manifest all God has for you right then. Change is constant and ever moving. We should be, too. Always remember, no matter what, share that unique smile with yourself first and then others that cross your path today.

*I'm so glad
I live in a world
where there are seasons!*

Now is the time to get quiet before God and pray. No matter what season you are in at this very moment write a daily encouragement to yourself to get you through this season of your life.

_____

_____

_____

_____

_____

_____

_____

_____

_____

_____

_____

_____

_____

_____

Date

Live a Life in Full Bloom

We must see our lives as a full bloom from beginning to end. A bloom does not start out beautiful. It is hidden deep beneath the surface until it is nurtured and cared for by nature and ready to sprout forth. Most of the work is done in secret where no one can see the process or speak against it. You could see it as almost forgotten until one day it sprouts. We must see our lives the same way before we can fully bloom and become beautiful. The work must be done in secret away from others. There is work to be done in your life and a nurturing from the Holy Spirit must consume your seed so that you can bloom in purpose. Don't rush the process of your blooming because every step is necessary for what is to come. We must be changed from the inside out and this is not easy. Just as the bloom has to break through the dirt and grass, we too, must break through everything coming against us to hinder us from becoming a full bloom. Don't allow anyone to pick you before your time. Make sure your roots run deep in the Word of God and you have a firm foundation. When the time is right you will begin to grow and break through to show the beauty of your full bloom. You are beautiful from the inside out and it's time to get in a secret and work on you. The Lord is waiting to see your full bloom because He knows that His creation is beautiful. Always remember, no matter what, share that unique smile with yourself first and then others that cross your path today.

In order to live life in full bloom, we must bloom where we are planted.

Now is the time to get quiet before God and pray. Write a prayer for God to keep your roots deep and strong so you can bloom where He has planted you for such a time as this. Be truthful with yourself. This is between you and God.

_____

_____

_____

_____

_____

_____

_____

_____

_____

_____

_____

_____

_____

_____

Date

Don't Give In

Don't give up just because life is beating you down. This life we walk every day is not easy, but one thing for sure, it's not impossible. Keep your head above the mess and the struggles and you will get through. Our storms are here to make us stronger and wiser. Don't just go through the storms, but make sure you learn something in the storms so that you may encourage yourself and others who may be going through. Live your life to encourage others. Life is precious and meant to be lived in peace, love and joy. Stay focused today on your purpose and make sure whatever you are going through, don't "wear it" on your face. You've got this and not only you, but we've got this together. Always remember, no matter what, share that unique smile with yourself first and then others that cross your path today.

However bad life may seem,
where there is life there is Hope!

Now is the time to get quiet before God and pray. Write a prayer that you can pray daily that will strengthen you to keep going and not give up. This is between you and God.

_____

_____

_____

_____

_____

_____

_____

_____

_____

_____

_____

_____

_____

_____

Date

Invest in Yourself

The past couple of weeks I have been refocusing my outlook on life. Getting back on the highway of purpose that was created just for me. Sometimes we get off track in our lives. Just know that it's okay. We are not perfect and we will stumble. An important thing to know is how to get up: pull yourself up by your boot straps, dust yourself off and get back on that path toward your purpose. Everyone is not meant to travel your path of purpose and people will have to go their own way. It won't be easy and it may hurt, but it is necessary to shake off the people and baggage that are slowing you down. You have a certain pace to keep up with on your path of purpose and you must endure. So, walk lightly on your path and invest in yourself every day, even if the investment is small. In time, with prayer, patience, perseverance and endurance you will go further and see a great return. Always remember, no matter what, share that unique smile with yourself first and then others that cross your path today.

Women who Invest in themselves go Further.

Now is the time to get quiet before God and pray. Write a prayer and meditate asking God to show you how to invest in yourself daily.

_____

_____

_____

_____

_____

_____

_____

_____

_____

_____

_____

_____

_____

_____

_____

_____

_____

_____

_____

Date

Step Forward

Make sure that every day you wake up there is a goal to step forward and progress. Wherever you are in your life there is always room for growth: spiritually, mentally or physically. Don't be afraid to take that step of faith into the unknown because you never know what opportunities await you on the other side. It's time to move forward in your life. Do something each day that you think is impossible and watch what happens. Don't become complacent where you are because life is too short to just be stagnant. Get up, pray for direction and move closer to your purpose! Take a step forward and refuse to go backward. It only gets better when you are moving forward in your life. I believe in progress and I know for a fact you got this. Make today the best one yet and enjoy this day to the fullest without hesitation. Always remember, no matter what, share that unique smile with yourself first and then others that cross your path today.

Everyday we wake up we are given two choices:
Step forward into purpose, or Step back into comfort.

Make a list of how you are stepping forward out of your comfort zone. Goals can push you further along than moving forward blindly. Be truthful with yourself. This is between you and God.

Date

Press Your Way Through

Today is a new day and yesterday is gone never to return again. If your yesterday didn't go quite as planned and you had a few stumbles along the way, just know this day is not over because of yesterday. Get excited to know that we have a whole new day to press into our promises and make one step closer to reaching that goal. Today I challenge you to remain in purpose, pray with purpose, have faith with purpose and watch what God can do. Just remember we have to press in order for something to change. Don't sit around waiting for something to happen in your life. Push fear aside, get up and keep on pressing 'til it happens. No one said our life's journey would be easy. Let's link arms, support and encourage one another because we all need each other. Have a wonderful and productive day in purpose. Always remember, no matter what, share that unique smile with yourself first and then others that cross your path today.

Press harder than yesterday if you want a different tomorrow.

Ask yourself what is holding you back from moving forwarded? It is time for you to get quiet and meditate and seek God for your breakthrough. Make a list of your hindrances and what it will take to press through. Be truthful with yourself. This is between you and God.

_____

_____

_____

_____

_____

_____

_____

_____

_____

_____

_____

_____

_____

Date

Take It Back

You know the Lord has made a promise to each and every one of us: "So I will restore to you the years that the swarming locust has eaten" (Joel 2:25). Stop allowing the enemy to take your peace, take your faith, take your joy, take your family, take your health, and take your finances. You need to understand who you are in Christ Jesus and Greater is on the inside of you. It's time to stand bold with a Holy confidence and know that, "no weapon that is formed against thee shall prosper; and every tongue that shall rise against thee in judgment thou shalt condemn. "(Is. 54:17a)" It's time to take back your life and live life the way it is supposed to be lived: in the fullness of Christ Jesus where love, peace and joy can overflow. I caution you not to end this year the way you entered.

You see, we have had enough opportunity to grow in the promises and knowledge of the Lord. We have had enough opportunity this year to exercise our faith in Christ Jesus. Stop looking and getting distracted by your fleshly vision and fix your vision on the spiritual things of God. Stop allowing unforgiveness to take root and dwell in your heart. It's time to uproot the spirit of unforgiveness and plant seeds of love in your heart that can water and grow so that it overflows from the inside out. We need to get serious about our purpose and the Word of God in our lives. Now is the time to look at every area of your life and examine yourself and ask as God asked Ezekiel, "Can these bones live?" (Ez. 37:1-14). Start to speak life to your dry and dead situations that look impossible and watch the shaking, moving and the coming together of the areas in your life. Start to breathe life once again. Get up, pray, fast, and praise your way to the next spiritual level in your life. We must put an action to our faith and listen for that still small voice to instruct us. Then, we may ask, "Lord what would You have me to do?"

Better days are ahead of us and we must be ready at all times to fight spiritually for our purpose that is designed specifically for each and every one of us. It's time to walk with God and stop walking against God. Quit straddling the fence and decide today which side of the fence you will stand on. No matter where you are in your life, it's not too late to change course and walk in your purpose. I pray you have a wonderful and blessed day. Be blessed and carry on!!! Always remember, no matter what, share that unique smile with yourself first and then others that cross your path today.

Journal Time

Start your day off by writing down a simple prayer that can carry you through the rest of the day and restore what has already been stolen in your life.

_____

_____

_____

_____

_____

_____

_____

_____

_____

_____

_____

_____

_____

_____

_____
Date

Start Today, Right Now & Make It Happen

It's time to stop dreaming and wishing and make your desires a reality. Stop procrastinating because you don't believe you can do it or achieve it. Make it a goal today to focus on what matters and what you can truly achieve. Take one step and day at a time and make it happen. Don't wait to look back when you are older and wish your life had been different. Life isn't perfect and you will have failures. Just make sure your successes outweigh your failures. This happens when you make an effort to not quit and you keep moving forward to what you desire your life to be.

There is no better day than today to make it happen. Don't hesitate another day! If there is a goal that you are working toward, take a step today to make it happen. Don't be afraid. Step out to do it! Time waits for no one and life is too short to hesitate. Stop wishing and wanting and get busy making it happen. Start today! Always remember, no matter what, share that unique smile with yourself first and then others that cross your path today.

Stop procrastinating and make it happen because the clock is ticking.

Make a list of goals that you need to accomplish to push you further than where you are right now.

_____

_____

_____

_____

_____

_____

_____

_____

_____

_____

_____

_____

_____

_____

_____

Date

Make Your Move

If you haven't taken the first step, then it's time to start.

GET UP & MAKE YOUR MOVE:

Do something that you thought was impossible.

It's not impossible to attain the possible.

The only thing you need to do is

GET OUT OF YOUR OWN WAY & REACH.

When you get past your own fears and reach, anything is possible for you. Often, we are the one in our own way of reaching toward our purpose and our own happiness in life.

STOP being afraid of the climb and reach for the possible of your purpose in life. Don't ever stop. Follow through and reach your true potential.

YOU GOT THIS!

Always remember, no matter what, share that unique smile with yourself first and then others that cross your path today.

*Don't be afraid it's time
to make your move.*

It's time to get before God and listen for Him to speak the strategy for your life and write the plan He gives you. After that make a list of the moves you need to make to push you forward into your purpose.

_____

_____

_____

_____

_____

_____

_____

_____

_____

_____

_____

_____

_____

_____

Date

Hit Reset

Life is a huge lesson with major learning opportunities. If we would slow down and take the time to learn the lesson and apply the lesson, life would be better. This means we could live life the way it was meant to be lived and enjoy life on our journey. In order for us to get a grip on our lives we must push the reset button and be still. In order for our lives to reset correctly, it means we need to get away from everyone and every situation. Don't go to the familiar when you get away, go somewhere that is quiet and peaceful where you can be still, listen and start the reset process. I am so thankful that our lives come with a reset button. Start to enjoy your life, press through the rough patches along the journey because in the end, it will be all worth it.

God wants me to tell you, "Be not discouraged but continue on in My will and plan for your life. This life is not easy, but remember, it is not impossible. I have given you everything on the inside that you will ever need to walk this journey. It's time to get up and begin your journey and stay in step with my steps and you will be ok. No matter what comes your way, I am right beside you to get you through. Repent and reset when the time comes for that necessary step and do not stay there, but keep moving forward. Your life has meaning and purpose because you are My child and I take care of My own. My sheep will not be lost, but remain in Me and I in them. Carry on my child and reset your purpose and plan in My will for your life." Always remember, no matter what, share that unique smile with yourself first and then others that cross your path today.

Push that reset button and make it happen because now is the time for greatness.

Now is the time to get quiet before God and pray. Write a prayer to ask God to show you what needs to be reset in your life. Be truthful with yourself. This is between you and God.

_____

_____

_____

_____

_____

_____

_____

_____

_____

_____

_____

_____

_____

_____

_____

_____

_____

_____
Date

A Life Refreshed

God will send you a refresher and an encourager! It's time to move out and move on, but I will not go at it alone. My life may feel broken and unsure right now, but I am holding on and believing that My God will send me peace in the midst of this storm. (*God is our refuge and strength, a very present help in trouble. Psalm 46:1*) I am believing and walking by faith that God will send someone into my life that I may glean from and continue to walk this journey. Just like Naomi was assigned to Ruth, I am confident that the Lord has assigned someone to me as well, who will be that refreshing, truthful, encouraging and wise voice that I need during these times. My life is going to be restored and filled with vision, focus and determination to press. God sees, knows and feels every one of my hurts, my desires, my confusion, my downcast spirit, and He is waiting to restore me. He is sending me a way of escape to get me through. Life is not meant to go at it alone all the time, He wants us to link up because there is strength and power in numbers. The key is, we must be on the same page with the same mindset and heart for the same purpose as Jesus. It is getting better, I truly must believe this. Always remember, no matter what, share that unique smile with yourself first and then others that cross your path today.

A life refreshed is a life destined for purpose.

Now is the time to get quiet before God and pray. Write a confession for God to refresh every area of your life that needs refreshing. Be truthful with yourself. This is between you and God.

_____

_____

_____

_____

_____

_____

_____

_____

_____

_____

_____

_____

_____

_____

_____

Date

New Week, New Focus

I pray that you are waking up with a new outlook for the week. New goals to accomplish this week. Some of us dread the start of a new week and wish for the weekend to return, but last week is gone never to return again. We need to look at the beginning of a new week as motivation to the start of something great on the horizon. The world is still turning, and people are still at unrest, but women of God need to be the game-changers. We need to get up and focus on our purpose of who and whose we are. It's not time to lay in our sorrows, discouragement, and disappointments. The time is now to get up and be confident in our purpose of why we were created. Don't be moved this day, if something doesn't go quite as planned. Control those emotions that can so easily become off balance because you are better than that. Add a little forgiveness to your goals today and find a situation that needs to be forgiven. You might not need to look far because sometimes we need to forgive who we look in the mirror at every morning. Sprinkle some joy on that heart this morning so that it can begin to have a bubbling joy that rises out of the depths of your soul. Why so downcast oh my soul? If you have breath this morning you definitely have something to be joyful about. The Bible says to make a joyful noise and now is the time to make that joyful noise. Don't think it strange you are still here because there is a purpose that needs to be fulfilled. If you are unsure of that purpose, seek God and allow Him to show you your purpose and how to walk in your purpose as He has planned. You are a woman of purpose beautifully created in the image of God. Now get up and walk in that beautiful confidence that is on the inside of you. Always remember, no matter what, share that unique smile with yourself first and then others that cross your path today.

*Stay focused because,
the best is yet to come.*

Make a priority list for the new week what you need to focus on spiritually, physically and mentally.

_____

_____

_____

_____

_____

_____

_____

_____

_____

_____

_____

_____

_____

_____

_____

Date

New Mercies Coming My Way

God's mercies are new every morning. We sometimes will take scriptures and change the words around to fit where we are at that point and time in our lives. One of the scriptures we have done this for is Lamentations 3:22. We say, "God's mercies are new every morning." When in fact what is new every morning is God's compassion. You see mercy is an act of forgiveness for one's harsh treatment, but compassion is an action of sympathy when in distress and works to alleviate it. Which would you want in your life right now? If you ask me I will want both and we need both in which this world we live in, but to know that God's compassion towards me, towards you are new every morning gives me hope for a new day. This means that no matter what I went through that day, how I acted, how a situation rose-up, how I felt like I failed just all the daily stuff I had to shuffle through. That when I close my eyes say a prayer sleep that night that God is already preparing me for the next day. You see while we sleep His mercy is working in and through us because when that time comes, and He nudges us to wake up it is time that a whole new day of compassion rest upon us and begins again. Why? Because He knows that we will need to be alleviated at some point and time from the distress. Our God loves us unconditionally and has a new whole day full of compassion for us. How exciting is that? Don't leave off the next scripture. When our feet cross that threshold of our home and we step outside of our homes our controlled environment into an uncontrolled environment we will need a portion of the Lord with us; so that, we will have a daily hope in the Lord for the day. We can get through each day knowing that we have a day full of mercy and compassion shown to us through Christ Jesus. One key element here is daily also to not forget to show that same mercy and compassion to others. Always remember, no matter what, share that unique smile with yourself first and then others that cross your path today.

Have a Blessed New Day!

Now is the time to get quiet before God and pray. Write a confession for God to give you new mercies daily. Be truthful with yourself. This is between you and God.

_____

_____

_____

_____

_____

_____

_____

_____

_____

_____

_____

_____

_____

_____

_____

_____

_____

_____

_____

_____
Date

Daily Prayers

Freedom from Rejection

Dear Heavenly Father,

I come before You this day thanking and praising You for who You are in my life. I am Your daughter and You are my Abba Father. I humbly bow my heart, spirit, soul and body to You and I renounce, uproot and tear down the spirit of rejection. Rejection will not and cannot survive in my spirit. I will no longer feed and nurture the spirit of rejection in my life or continue to pass it on to my children. I am whole and complete in Christ Jesus. I walk with a spiritual confidence knowing that I belong and have a place in the Kingdom of Christ Jesus. I shall be anxious for nothing, but I shall by prayer and supplication have a confidence so rooted in my Heavenly Father that rejection does not exist in my eyes. I surround myself with confidence, love, joy and peace. I put an ax to the root of rejection and uproot it out of my heart. I will plant love in place of rejection and walk it out daily. Peace and love will surround my heart, mind and soul every day and protect me from the spirit of rejection. I will truly love myself and others from the inside out. I will know and have an understanding of true love. I will not fear man or who I am because my God has created me in His image after His likeness. The Holy Spirit will strengthen my inner man so that I will not fall into the grips of rejection. When I am tempted and rejection comes and knocks on my door, I will have a boldness to not accept that spirit back into my life. From this day forth I will not and cannot walk in withdrawal, suspicion or social shyness. I will not neglect to show kindness to strangers or those around me because I know who and whose I am. I shall not be a grumbler, nor be dissatisfied or rebellious, following my own sinful desires. I shall not be a loud boaster, showing favoritism to gain advantage. I want to be like a tree that bears good fruit for the Kingdom of God. I thank You and praise You. In Jesus' Name, Amen.

Rejection doesn't mean you aren't good enough; it means the other person failed to notice what you have to offer.
-Mark Amend

A Mother's Strength

Dear Heavenly Father,

I come before You this day thanking and praising You for who You are in my life. Today I come before you with an open heart and a request for strength and peace in my life as a mother. I want to repent for where I have not been the mother that you have desired me to be. At times as a mother I get weary and overwhelmed, but I know deep down that you have so much more for me to give back to my children. I need right now a motherly fresh encounter as only You can give my spirit, Lord God. I ask You to start working on my heart and mind right now to wash over me and cleanse me from the crown of my head to the souls of my feet. Teach me Lord how to be a Godly mother that knows when and how to pray over her children. Make my heart prepared as a dwelling place for You to reside and live daily without reservation. Show me and reveal to me the type of mother You desire me to be. I believe with my whole heart that there is so much more You have in store for me as a mother and I invite You to start working on me right now. I know and understand that change does not happen overnight and it is a process, but I want You to know I am ready to start right where I am. I understand that I may take two steps back, but You are right beside me to push me many more steps ahead. I thank you for walking with me daily even when I don't deserve it and most of all, being patient with me. I thank You for motherhood in my life. My prayer is that my family will see love, peace and patience working in me. Thank You Lord for showing me love so that I can overflow that same love upon my family. In Jesus' Name, Amen.

She watches over the ways of her household,

And does not eat the bread of idleness.

Her children rise up and call her blessed;

Proverbs 31: 27-28

Pressed on Every Side

Lord, what is it that overwhelms me?
I am pressed on every side in every area of my life.
Nothing seems to be going quite as planned.
Where did it all go wrong?
Where did I manage to fail in my life?
My children are completely out of control.
What have I done to deserve this?

Life will often bring us to a place to ask these questions and more, but we must remember what God has to say:

My child, you must understand that life will throw everything at you sometimes all at once, but that does not mean you have done anything to deserve this. You must understand that My plan for you is beyond what you can see. There is no degree or certificate required for you to carry out my plan. I have stamped and sealed you with My approval for what you will and have gone through. My plan is to prosper you and show you an expected end that I have designed for your life. Yes, trials, stressors and heartaches will come because the life I have chosen for you is not easy. All that I have asked of you is that you walk in the plan I have prepared for you by praying daily, studying My word and holding My promises in your heart. I have given you the blueprint for this journey even how to get over, around and through the obstacles that come your way. You don't need to look to the right or the left. Don't look at how you think it should be. Don't look at what others may or may not be doing. Don't look at the failures or disappointments. Don't even look at the good times. I need you to focus your eyes up on Me and don't look down. Start to prepare yourself for whatever may be coming and get rooted in Me so that you can press your way through. Watch the seasons of your life, study to show thyself approved unto God so that you may be ready and know when, where and how to use what I have given you to get through. Live your life to the fullest everyday no matter what is being thrown at you. Always know that I have not left you or forsaken you. Sometimes my silence to you is Me working behind the scenes. You won't always see what is going on in the background, but just know when the time is right, the plan I am working on will come together. Always keep love, peace and joy in your heart and pass it on to others also that may be going through at the same time. You see, My Word will not fail and it is there as a weapon for you to use at just the right time. Fear not, My child, for your journey is strategically designed just for you. There are no detours, so stay the course and I will meet you at the beginning, middle and most of all, at the end.

Thou shalt increase my greatness, and comfort me on every side.
Psalm 71: 21

Cleanse Me Completely

Dear Heavenly Father,

I come humbly now before Your throne of repentance and ask You to forgive me from the crown of my head to the soles of my feet. I repent of any sin that has taken root in my life; whether it was an ungodly conversation, something I let enter my body, some place I should not have gone, something I watched, etc. Lord, if there is any area of my life that needs to be cleaned up and refocused, show me and reveal to me those areas. I need You to completely wash, scrub and burn up those areas in my life that are not of You. I want to walk upright and in the perfect plan you have prepared for my life this day. I understand and know that I will have to fight to remain in the place where You have prepared for me, and I am willing to do just that. May peace, patience, joy and love overflow and overtake me in the name of Jesus as I go through the cleansing process. I will walk before You daily with a repentant heart. I thank You that You will be right by my side revealing to me when I need to make that turn and get back on track. Thank You, Lord, for hearing my heart's desire for a cleansing. In Jesus' Name, Amen.

Wash me thoroughly from my iniquity,
And cleanse me from my sin.

Psalm 51:2

A Heart of Thanks

Dear Heavenly Father,

I come before Your throne of grace thanking and praising You for who You are in my life. I thank You for leading and guiding me daily every step of the way and speaking to me daily in that still small voice. I come before You with a heart of thanksgiving not for material things, but for the spiritual blessing You show to me daily even when I don't recognize it. You are an almighty and powerful God and there is none like You. You hold the beginning and You hold the end and know all things pertaining to me. You know my coming and my going. You just Are! I pray that You continue to give me a heart of love and understanding. I have a true heart's desire to be complete in You, which means I am firmly rooted and built up in You, no wavering or looking back, but staying focused on You and always looking up to where my help comes from. Thank You for keeping me focused on You. In Jesus' Name, Amen.

A pure heart is a thankful heart.

Keep Me Patient

Dear Heavenly Father,

I stand before You continually broken and poured out for You. Lord, it gets hard at times to see family members, friends or just people in general struggling and unhappy when you know what a powerhouse they would be in Your Kingdom. I understand people have seen me the same way, but God, I thank You for breaking me and putting me right where You wanted me to be for such a time as this. I love You so much Lord and I know now in my heart of hearts, all You want is what is best for Your daughter. You know when, where and how that strength and boldness will be released in and over my life. I just need to be ready and keep my eyes, ears and mind ever before you and attentive to Your voice. "Here I am Lord, send me," should be my daily confession. I pray that You will continue to cleanse and renew my heart and mind daily and draw me even closer to You. Your presence in my life is not only where I need to be, but where I desire and want to be. If You lead me, Lord, I will obey and follow You. As long as I am in your presence, You will give me peace and patience that surpasses all understanding. Gird me up and strengthen me for the journey ahead. In Jesus' Name, Amen.

I waited patiently for the Lord;
And He inclined to me,
And heard my cry.
Psalm 40:1

May Love Abide

Dear Heavenly Father,

I thank You for being love and showing love in my life daily. I pray that my heart will be one of love that overflows onto everyone that I pass. I pray that I can show genuine love even if it doesn't come back in return. Show me where I have been unloving towards others and teach me how to turn that into a genuine heart of love. I want to be able to love the unlovable with nothing in return. I thank You for giving me wisdom in my life and encouragement to help and lift up someone who needs it. I pray You will add a tender and loving heart to my life that can draw others and help change a life. Where I have been hurt, I pray you will heal my wounds and cover them with your love so that when the healing comes, love has taken root. I pray You will burn up any stubborn, unloving ways that have taken root in my heart. I want to be like You, loving and sincere towards all men. Mold me and make me in love and sincerity. In Jesus' Name, Amen.

And now abide faith, hope, love,
these three; but the greatest
of these is love.

1 Corinthians 13:13

Blessings Overflowing

Dear Heavenly Father,

I come before You this day with a pure heart and a open and clear mind to hear from You, Lord. I pray for an abundance of peace and joy to overflow me from the inside out. I thank You for clarity in my life this day and a new start to what You are about to bless me with. I am a child of the Most High God and I walk with assurance and confidence. I pray that You will continue to lead and guide my life and every step I take. I am asking and believing by faith that everything the enemy has stolen or destroyed, that it will be returned one-hundred fold. I am believing that this is my year and season to see the power of God move on my behalf and in every area of my life spiritually, physically and financially, and also in the lives of my family members. I thank You in advance for what You are about to do and for what You have already done. I will continue to praise and worship You from the depths of my soul. I come before You with an open heart so that You may cleanse me from the crown of my head to the soles of my feet. Be it according to Your Word. Today is a wonderful and prosperous day in You, Christ Jesus. I love You Lord and I thank You for being ever so patient, loving and kind towards me. Thanking You for hearing me. In Jesus' Name, Amen.

Blessings pouring out in your life.
A shifting is coming in your direction.
Every situation is getting better
All things are aligning.
Blessings are coming.

Daily Thanks

Dear Heavenly Father,

I thank You for allowing me to see another day and experience Your awesome presence this day. I am believing by faith that no matter what today brings it will be a wonderful day. I thank You for yesterday and all my experiences and I look forward for what today holds. May I be a beacon of light for someone today who I may come in contact with. I pray that the joy of the Lord and the love of the Lord overtake me and flow through me from the inside out. May I radiate Your love today, Lord. Overflow me this day with Your blessing and promises. Keep me focused on the path You have designed just for me and if I get off track, give me a gentle nudge to put me in the right direction. I am Your vessel ready to be used by You. Cleanse me from the inside out and from the crown of my head to the soles of my feet. I pray Lord that You will abide in me and I in You. Quiet my spirit so that I may hear from You when You speak to me in that still small voice. I thank You in advance for the doors that have been opened and the ones that have been unlocked by You. I praise and worship You from the depths of my soul. Put a new song in my heart and a dance upon my feet. Thank You Lord. I am just full of thanks with a side of gratitude for who You are in my life. Keep my mind young and renewed so that I can retain all You have given me. Take fear out of my life and replace it with a strong unwavering faith. I see my future and I am ready to take hold of it. I thank You and love you. In Jesus' Name, Amen.

*Gratitude turns what
we have into enough.*

Personal Reflection

This is your personal reflection time. A time to reflect on who and who's you are and where you desire to be in your life right now. Just begin to write and let God pour into you so that you can over flow on this page.

_____

_____

_____

_____

_____

_____

_____

_____

_____

_____

_____

_____

_____

_____

_____

_____

_____

_____

_____

_____

Date

This is your personal reflection time. A time to reflect on who and who's you are and where you desire to be in your life right now. Just begin to write and let God pour into you so that you can over flow on this page.

_____

_____

_____

_____

_____

_____

_____

_____

_____

_____

_____

_____

_____

_____

_____

_____

_____

_____

Date

From the Author

Although my life has been filled with plenty of ups and downs, ins and outs, and roundabouts, here I am!

I'm a daughter of the most amazing parents, Pastor Phil & Pastor Betty, and words cannot fully convey my gratitude to and for them. As parents, they demonstrated the patience of Job when raising me!

To everything there is a season, a time for every purpose under heaven. By God's grace in His purpose, I experience life, love and laughter with the most incredible best friend, Antwann. Our journey since high school has been joyful, challenging, and downright painful to say the least, but we have endured and continue to thrive every day. I could never ask for anyone more supportive and encouraging.

I'm a mother of two wonderful young men, Gabriel and Jeremiah, and grandmother to two precious little ones, Trinity and Hayden. They bring me joy over and over again. My favorite family tradition is sitting around talking and laughing—enjoying the comforts of home.

Most of all, my greatest joy and satisfaction is being a daughter of The Most High! I love the Lord with all my heart, mind and soul.

Be Blessed!

Andrea Arnold